## WHAT OTHERS ARE SAYING ABOUT

# The Courier Air Travel Handbook

"If you're looking for a bottom-dollar flight, courier trips can't be beat. For valuable information, check out *The Courier Air Travel Handbook* by Mark Field."
— **Cosmopolitan Magazine**

"*The Courier Air Travel Handbook* will help you stretch your travel budget."
— **Off Duty Military Magazine**

"Fly to Worldwide Destinations for as little as $99 roundtrip, or even free."
— **Transitions Abroad Magazine**

"The Courier's Bible . . ."
— **The Midwest Book Review**

"To sort out fact from fiction about courier travel, get *The Courier Air Travel Handbook.*"
— **The Houston Chronicle**

"The courier company pays most or all of your airfare."
— **The Seattle Times**

"Colossal savings on airfare are offered to air couriers."
— **Fodor's Travel Publications**

"Go as a courier, and save major bucks on a flight."
— **Newsday**

"This book explains how you can fly around the world for next to nothing."
— **The Arizona Republic**

"As a courier, fly three times as far at about 25 percent of the cost. The bargains are extreme."
— **The San Francisco Chronicle**

"A handy guide to the ins and outs of courier travel is *The Courier Air Travel Handbook* by Mark I. Field."
— **The Chicago Sun Times**

# Timeless Travel Quotes

I travel not to go anywhere, but to go. I travel for travel's sake. The great affair is to move.

—*Robert Louis Stevenson*
*1850–1894*


Travel, in the younger sort, is a part of education; in the elder, a part of experience.

—*Francis Bacon*
*1561–1626*


Travel is one way of lengthening life, at least in appearance.

—*Benjamin Franklin*
*1706–1790*


Il faut être toujours botté et prêt à partir. (One should always have one's boots on and be ready to leave.)

—*Michel de Montaigne*
*1533–1592*

# THE COURIER AIR TRAVEL HANDBOOK

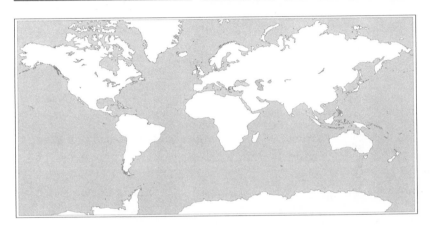

**Learn How to Travel Worldwide for Next to Nothing**

Mark I. Field

**Perpetual Press
Lansing, Michigan**

*Field Travel Guides*
*An Innovative Travel Series*

# The Courier Air Travel Handbook

Printed in the United States of America
Book cover design by Bob Silverman
Interior design and layout by Julia M. Lauer, Tammy Thornas, Brenda Spoonemore, and Andrew Ratshin
Cover photos courtesy of Andy M. Clarke and Kristen C. Weiss
7th edition Project Manager: Kevin Hile
7th edition Research Editor: Thomas J. Votteler
7th edition Research Assistants: Eileen Benson and Betsie Janson
7th edition Production/Layout: Peter Myers


First printing–July 1990
Second printing–August 1991–2nd edition
Third printing–November 1991
Fourth printing–December 1991
Fifth printing–February 1992
Sixth printing–May 1992–3rd edition
Seventh printing–October 1992
Eighth printing–May 1993
Ninth printing–October 1993–4th edition
Tenth printing–June 1994
Eleventh printing–February 1996–5th edition
Twelfth printing–June 1996–6th edition
Thirteenth printing–March 1998–7th edition


ISBN 1-881199-99-1


Published by:
Perpetual Press
P.O. Box 30414
Lansing, MI 48909-7914


Distributed to the Book Trade by:
Ingram Book Company at (800) 937-8000


Published in Europe by Uitgeverij Het Spectrum BV.

# About The Author

*The author at Grand Canyon National Park*

Mark I. Field is an avid world traveler. He is originally from New York City and now makes his home in Arizona, where he is a marketing executive. Prior to attending college, he spent eight years in the Navy serving on submarines, where he was part of the Space Shuttle Challenger Recovery Operation and served in Military Intelligence. He is a graduate of the University of Arizona with a degree in business economics and attended The American Graduate School of International Management.

Mark was inspired to write this book because during his travels he encountered so many people who knew little or nothing about courier travel. He felt more people would have the opportunity to travel if they only knew about this concept. "The ability to travel should not be decided by one's financial position," he asserts. On one of his trips Mark backpacked throughout Europe on an extremely limited budget ... and had the time of his life. Besides travel, Mark also enjoys golf, tennis, and jogging.

# Dedication

*This book is dedicated to my mother, Betty Lou Field, who inspired in me a desire to travel and see the world.*

# Acknowledgments

*The author wishes to thank the following people:*

- Julia M. Lauer for her creative ability.
- Jeffrey J. Leslie for his continued support and assistance.
- Dan Poynter for his inspiration and guidance.
- Tammy Thornas for her commitment and tireless dedication.
- Kristen C. Weiss for her exceptional research and marketing ability.
- Craig Evans for his outstanding research dedication.
- Heidi Robinson for her thorough proofreading and layout support.
- Jennifer DuBois and Thom Votteler for project management.

# Contents

# A NOTE ON PRICES AND DESTINATIONS

The courier industry, like the travel industry, changes constantly. Every effort has been made to provide the reader with accurate information, and all the information in this book is based on the best information available at the time of publication.

This book is updated at each printing. This ensures the most current information is available to the reader. This seventh edition is completely revised from cover to cover.

Prices, destinations, phone numbers, and other pertinent information in this book are subject to change. It is important to realize that courier companies may go out of business, change their policies concerning onboard couriers, or simply change their phone numbers.

If you come across any new information, please write to me in care of the publisher. If I include it in the next edition of this book, I will acknowledge your contribution and send you a free copy of the book.

—*Mark I. Field*

# COMMON QUESTIONS AND ANSWERS ABOUT COURIER TRAVEL

**Q: Who can travel as a courier?**

    A:  Anyone who is over the age of 18 and has a valid passport. You need not be a citizen of the country in which the courier flights originate. If you are a traveler, student, teacher, retiree, businessperson, adventurer, or just interested in saving money, you're an ideal candidate for courier travel.

**Q: Will I have to transport anything illegal?**

    A:  Absolutely not. The courier industry is a respectable industry.

**Q: What will I have to transport?**

    A:  The types of items that you will transport include documents, files, boxes, computer disks, contracts, and so on. You will *not* have to load the material. The courier company takes care of that on both ends.

**Q: What are the benefits of courier travel?**

    A:  The money you save. As a courier, you will only pay a small percentage of the cost of the plane ticket.

**Q: Can I pay the airline money to take an extra bag?**

    A:  Most airlines will allow you to take extra baggage if you pay an additional baggage charge, but it may or may not be worth the extra money. If you must take your entire wardrobe, then courier travel may not be for you. In that case, give this book to a friend!

# WORLDWIDE COURIER DESTINATIONS

| | | | | | |
|---|---|---|---|---|---|
| 1. | Amman | 15. | Cairo | 29. | Istanbul |
| 2. | Amsterdam | 16. | Cape Town | 30. | Jakarta |
| 3. | Athens | 17. | Caracas | 31. | Jamaica |
| 4. | Auckland | 18. | Chicago | 32. | Johannesburg |
| 5. | Bahrain | 19. | Copenhagen | 33. | Kuala Lumpur |
| 6. | Bali | 20. | Dubai | 34. | La Paz |
| 7. | Bangkok | 21. | Dublin | 35. | Larnaca |
| 8. | Beijing | 22. | Frankfurt | 36. | Lima |
| 9. | Boston | 23. | Gabarone | 37. | Lisbon |
| 10. | Brisbane | 24. | Geneva | 38. | London |
| 11. | Brussels | 25. | Guatamala City | 39. | Los Angeles |
| 12. | Budapest | 26. | Harare | 40. | Madrid |
| 13. | Buenos Aires | 27. | Hong Kong | 41. | Managua |
| 14. | Cairns | 28. | Honolulu | 42. | Manila |

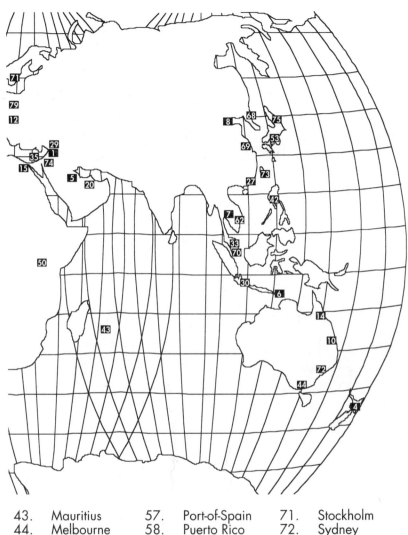

| | | | |
|---|---|---|---|
| 43. | Mauritius | 57. | Port-of-Spain |
| 44. | Melbourne | 58. | Puerto Rico |
| 45. | Mexico City | 59. | Quito |
| 46. | Miami | 60. | Rio de Janeiro |
| 47. | Milan | 61. | Rome |
| 48. | Montevideo | 62. | Saigon |
| 49. | Montreal | 63. | San Francisco |
| 50. | Nairobi | 64. | San Jose |
| 51. | Newark | 65. | Santiago |
| 52. | New York | 66. | Sao Paulo |
| 53. | Osaka | 67. | Seattle |
| 54. | Panama City | 68. | Seoul |
| 55. | Paris | 69. | Shanghai |
| 56. | Philadelphia | 70. | Singapore |

| | |
|---|---|
| 71. | Stockholm |
| 72. | Sydney |
| 73. | Taipei |
| 74. | Tel Aviv |
| 75. | Tokyo |
| 76. | Toronto |
| 77. | Vancouver |
| 78. | Vienna |
| 79. | Warsaw |
| 80. | Washington, DC |
| 81. | Zurich |

# HOW TO USE THIS GUIDE

## NEW YORK

### Air Facility

| Destination | Round trip/last-minute fare | Length of stay/Departure days |
|---|---|---|
| **Buenos Aires** | **$470/None** | **7–15 days; Mon–Thu, Sat** |
| **Caracas** | **$210/None** | **7–14 days; Mon–Thu, Sat** |
| **Montevideo** | **$480/None** | **7–15 days; Mon–Thu, Sat** |
| **Rio de Janiero** | **$405/$300** | **7–14 days; Mon–Thu, Sun** |
| **Santiago** | **$460/None** | **8–9 days; Mon–Thu, Sat** |
| **Sao Paulo** | **$395/$300** | **6–13 days; Mon–Thu, Sat** |

**Flights originating from:** New York
**Address:** 153-40 Rockaway Boulevard, Jamaica, NY 11434
**Phone:** (718) 712-1769
**Fax:** (718) 712-2597
**Toll-free number:** No
**Point of contact:** Marisa
**Times to call:** 9AM–4:30PM EST Mon–Fri
**Recorded information:** No
**Type of business:** Courier Company
**Conducting business since:** 1988
**Annual registration fee:** No
**Courier assignment length:** 1 to 2 weeks
**Luggage restrictions:** Carry-on only
**Frequent flyer mileage accrued:** Yes
**Airlines used:** Varig, United
**Return date flexibility:** No
**One-way tickets available:** No
**Cancellation phone list:** Yes
**Last-minute discounts:** Yes
**Additional non-courier travel services:** No
**Recommended advance reservations:** 2 months
**Earliest possible reservations:** 2 months
**Departure taxes:** $40 in cash
**Deposit:** No
**Method of payment:** Certified check; money order; cash
**Credit cards accepted:** No
**Comments:** Prices are slightly higher during summer months and in December. Air Facility depends on responsible people to act as couriers for them. If you cancel a flight last minute, they place you on a black list, and you will not be allowed to fly with them in the future. They are helpful and offer consistently inexpensive fares to South America.

*Courier company name:* The name under which the company conducts business

*Destination:* Cities to which the company offers courier flights

*R/T fare:* Standard round-trip fare offered by the courier company

*Last-minute fare:* Cheapest fare; flight usually departs in a couple days

*Length of stay/Departure days:* Information concerning how long the trip is and which days flights depart

*Flights originating from:* Cities from which the courier flights originate

*Address:* Location from which this office conducts business

*City/State/Zip:* City, state, and zip code from which this office conducts business

*Phone:* Phone number at which to call courier company

*Fax:* Fax number at which to fax courier company

*Toll-free number:* Toll-free number at which to call the company

*Point of contact:* Person to contact to help arrange courier flights

*Times to call:* General business hours or specific times outlined by the courier company

*Recorded information:* Recorded phone message providing courier flight availability, fares, and other information

*Type of business:* Courier company, courier broker, or travel agent

*Conducting business since:* Year in which the company began operations

*Annual registration fee:* Fee assigned by the courier company or broker

*Courier assignment length:* Length of stay

*Luggage restrictions:* Number of pieces of luggage allowed

*Frequent flyer mileage accrued:* Whether frequent flyer mileage goes to the traveler

*Airlines used:* Airlines that courier company flights are on

*Return date flexibility:* Whether you can change the return date

*One-way tickets available:* Restrictions of courier company concerning roundtrip or one way courier flights

*Cancellation phone list:* Whether the company will contact you if they have a cancellation

*Last-minute discounts:* Whether a company will offer a discounted fare covering flights with short notice

*Additional non-courier travel services:* Whether a company offers information on rental cars and other travel services

*Recommended advance reservations:* How far in advance you should call for your flight reservation

*Earliest possible reservations:* How far in advance you can call for your reservation

*Departure taxes:* Additional fees added to your courier flight

*Deposit:* Money courier companies ask you to put up to ensure you fulfill your obligation

*Method of payment:* How you can pay for your courier flight

*Credit cards accepted:* Whether the courier company will accept credit cards

*Comments:* Other miscellaneous information

# PART I

# ABOUT

# COURIER TRAVEL

What is a courier? A courier is a person who delivers something for someone. Couriers purchase reduced rate airline tickets from courier companies in exchange for accompanying cargo on a commercial airline. An air courier is an individual such as yourself who acts as the agent simply by occupying a seat on the plane and therefore permits the courier company to transport packages by air. Federal Express, UPS, and Emery are examples of air courier companies; however, they are large and own their own planes. There are literally hundreds of such companies in the world, though most of them are lesser known than Federal Express and UPS. The air courier companies in this book solicit members of the public to act as couriers for them. By acting as an air courier you allow the company to transport material by giving up the right to check in some or all of your luggage in exchange for a cheaper airfare.

Every year thousands of people travel around the world as couriers. This book will show you step-by-step how to become an air courier. You can begin today to travel to many exciting cities around the world for a fraction of the normal cost of airline tickets. Courier travel is one of the cheapest and simplest ways to travel around the world. How else can you travel from New York to London for $99 roundtrip or Los Angeles to Hong Kong for $150 roundtrip? This book will show you how you can travel worldwide for next to nothing or even free.

## WHO CAN TRAVEL AS AN AIR COURIER?

Courier travel is available to anyone, provided you are over the age of eighteen and have a valid passport. Courier travel is used by a wide variety of people, especially students, senior citizens, business travelers, adventurers, or just anyone interested in saving money. Senior citizens are becoming an increasingly important part of this industry, because many of them have the desire and time to travel. Courier travel is also an ideal method of travel for both students and teachers given their natural desire to travel and their ample free time.

## WHAT DO COURIER COMPANIES SHIP?

First, courier companies will not attempt to ship anything illegal. The items that you will transport may include documents, books, blueprints, supplies, equipment, checks, and so on. The material is similar to material shipped via other sources, such as Federal Express or UPS. The items tend to be time-sensitive. Simply put, it needs to get there quickly. It is important to know that the courier company will turn the material over to the airline, and they will retrieve the material upon completion of the flight. You, the courier, will usually never see or touch the actual shipment. What you actually carry is a manifest, which is a detailed list of cargo that the courier company is shipping. This is what you present to the customs officer upon arrival in a foreign country. It is because you never touch the material, that you, the courier, need not be bonded. Occasionally, there is a need for bonded couriers to deliver high-value items; however, most bonded couriers are professionals in the industry and tend to do this on a full-time basis. If you are interested in this line of employment, you should make this known to the courier company. However, this book is oriented toward the nonprofessional, leisure, or business traveler. As stated before, the companies listed in this book do not require bonding.

## WHY ARE COURIERS USED?

The use of courier companies is a cheaper and more efficient way to ship materials compared to traditional transportation methods, such as rail, truck, and air freight. The reason for this is that the courier companies ship the material as luggage on board commercial airlines. All passenger baggage is walked through customs, as opposed to unaccompanied shipments. This is the key behind courier travel.

Unaccompanied material can be detained by customs, often for over a week. This would add tremendous expense to the cost of transportation. Recently I sent a box of these books internationally through air freight, as opposed to using a courier service, only to have the books be delayed in storage by customs for ten days. Additionally, customs then charged the recipient of the books ten days worth of storage, which exceeded the cost of the shipment itself. Aside from the fact that the material shipped through courier companies tends to be cheaper for the consumer, it is also much more efficient for time-sensitive material. For example, daily sales reports might need to be transported from a branch office in New York to the firm's headquarters in London. Certain items cannot be faxed, such as original contracts, checks, and of course, bulky material.

One of my favorite examples of this is when a Hollywood film company was making a movie in London and left the lead actress's wig in Los Angeles. A courier company was used to transport the wig to London that same day. So you can see, there really is a need for courier service. Many people, including myself, have used this method of travel to see the world on a shoestring.

Often the courier company does not have anything to ship. This does not mean, however, that they do not still have a ticket to sell. Most courier companies buy their tickets for a flight every day for up to six months in advance. For example, one company in New York might purchase a ticket to Paris on an American Airlines flight that leaves at ten o'clock in the morning every day of the year. So if you buy a ticket for a flight to Paris three months in advance, the courier company will not know if they have anything to transport until a day or two before the flight. Even if the courier company has nothing to ship, the plane ticket has already been bought by the courier company and re-sold to you. This was the case on my recent flight to London. Given that my ticket only cost $250 roundtrip, I could not have gotten a better deal.

But why do courier companies need people to fly as couriers? All overseas flights must have a passenger for the checked luggage. This is a security issue. When you check in for a flight at Los Angeles International Airport or any other airport, the authorities check your baggage. The courier company must abide by these same rules.

You should be very careful when asked to transport a bag for somebody else, because you might not know what the contents may be. It is important to ensure that the material is thoroughly checked by the authorities and that you have a manifest. The courier company provides you with a manifest itemizing what is being transported.

Due to the fact that you will not touch the material, you are not responsible for it in case of damage during transport. It is the courier company's responsibility to ensure the material is packaged well and arrives intact. You are essentially just going along for the ride.

## WILL I HAVE TO TRANSPORT ANYTHING ILLEGAL?

A bsolutely not. This is the most common question I am asked about courier travel. All over the world, people have concerns about this question. I personally have traveled as a courier, and have met many other people who have had only good experiences when using this book as a guide. The companies in this book are reputable, and are used by thousands of people each and every year.

Travel as an air courier is safe. You will not be transporting anything illegal; this is a very respectable industry. When you contact a courier company to inquire about a particular flight, not only will they inform you of the airline that you will travel with, but they will often include a letter from that airline, indicating that this courier company is either the exclusive courier agent or one of the courier agents used by that airline. Again, all of the courier companies listed in this book are legitimate and reputable. Furthermore, they must be insured and bonded to operate in this industry.

There has been some negative publicity surrounding the term "courier." This is a broad term applied to many things; unfortunately it is sometimes applied to drug and contraband smuggling. This is not the case for courier companies listed in this book. These companies are reputable firms in good standing with the airlines.

However, courier companies start up, change names, change ownership, change phone numbers, change policies regarding onboard couriers, and change prices and destinations. If you come across a new courier company—one that is not listed in this book—use common sense to determine if it is a legitimate company. As more businesses expand into the international market, the greater the necessity for courier companies and agents called couriers. Additionally, as the speed of communication increases, the speed of transportation must keep pace. This is why the courier industry is expanding.

## WHAT ARE THE ECONOMICS OF COURIER TRAVEL?

T he economics behind the courier industry are quite simple. A courier company will purchase a roundtrip ticket in advance to an overseas destination. This ticket might cost the company $700 roundtrip. They, in turn, take orders to ship material for that day. A courier company will charge about $50 to deliver a small package overseas;

## FLIGHT PRICE COMPARISON

| Trip | Airlines | | Courier | |
|---|---|---|---|---|
| | Advance Purchase | Last Minute | Advance Purchase | Last Minute |
| New York–Rome | $1,191 | $1,611 | $220 | $99 |
| Los Angeles–London | $904 | $1,980 | $460 | $350 |
| Miami–Rio de Janeiro | $720 | $1,078 | $500 | $350 |
| San Francisco–Bangkok | $1,117 | $2,020 | $370 | $100 |
| Los Angeles–Sydney | $828 | $1,215 | $750 | $699 |
| Chicago–London | $725 | $1,700 | $450 | $350 |
| New York–London | $449 | $710 | $220 | $99 |
| New York–Paris | $535 | $1,498 | $250 | $99 |
| San Francisco–Singapore | $1,785 | $2,552 | $535 | $400 |
| New York–Madrid | $641 | $1,293 | $220 | $99 |
| Miami–Buenos Aires | $1,150 | $1,650 | $800 | $450 |
| New York–Rio de Janeiro | $1,183 | $1,790 | $405 | $300 |
| San Francisco–London | $897 | $2,194 | $335 | $100 |
| Washington, D.C.–London | $686 | $1,383 | $340 | $300 |
| New York–Singapore | $700 | $3,531 | $428 | $187 |
| New York–Johannesburg | $1,052 | $2,727 | $999 | $499 |
| Los Angeles–Hong Kong | $792 | $1,213 | $350 | $150 |

large, heavy, or expensive items can be delivered for an even higher price. The courier could generate up to $4,000 in revenue per flight.

The company then turns around and sells you their $700 roundtrip ticket for as low as $99. According to this example, the company would bring in roughly $3,350 in profit. This is the reason why they can afford to sell you the plane ticket so inexpensively.

The courier company offers the plane ticket to the general public at a discounted price in order to recoup some of their money. If the courier company cannot sell the ticket, or if they have a cancellation, then the ticket may be given away for free. This happens fairly often, as it is better for the company to take a loss on the $700 ticket than to send an employee who would have to be paid for his time and expenses. Simply put, it is in the best interest of the courier company to offer the ticket for sale to the general public. There are times when some courier companies are unable to locate people able and willing to fly to a particular city on a certain date. This is when the courier companies become desperate and ticket prices drop considerably.

A good example of this is when World Courier could not locate anyone to fly to Mexico City, and was forced to offer the ticket for free for over a two-month period. Another example is New York to Singapore for $150 roundtrip.

The price you pay for your ticket is simply a supply and demand dilemma. For example, the demand for airline tickets to Greece in the summer is high, while the supply is fixed; therefore, the price will rise. This is true with courier companies, commercial airlines, and the travel industry in general. So if you want to take a courier flight in the summer time, expect prices to be higher due to the increased number of people interested in flying and willing to do it. It is unlikely you will find the greatest savings during the summer. This is also true during the holidays. If you want to fly to Paris for Christmas, courier flights will be at a premium. However, even though the prices will be high relative to courier travel, they will still be less than commercial flights.

One way I am able to work around this problem is by attempting to travel off-season. Instead of flying to Greece in the summer, consider going to South America or Asia. However, often one country's low season is another country's high-season, and you can use this to your advantage. Australia's peak season is December through March—their summer, and our winter. This time of year is also a slow time for people willing to travel, both in Europe and in the United States. Therefore, you can expect inexpensive airline tickets to Australia during its high season.

Traveling as a courier is similar to traveling as a full-paying passenger—the only difference is the access to the information in this book and the price you pay. Couriers are sent on major airlines including United, Northwest, Delta, American, British Airways, Virgin, Lufthansa, Air France, Iberia, Cathay Pacific, and Singapore Airlines. As an air courier, you will be treated like any other passenger. The only difference will be that the person sitting next to you might be paying $500 more for their seat than you paid for yours.

Another common question I am asked is regarding frequent flyer mileage. It is true that most courier flights will give you frequent flyer mileage; however, there are occasions when the courier company, in order to get a low fare from the airline, will waive the right to frequent flyer mileage for that particular airline. Usually, when companies do not offer you the frequent flyer mileage, the ticket tends to be even more discounted than other courier flights. Attempt to obtain the frequent flyer mileage by requesting it from the courier company, and the airline even after the flight, if necessary.

Nobody will know that you are an air courier unless you tell them, and do tell them. It is a great conversation piece and gives you an added mystique. Usually when I travel, I strike up a conversation with someone in the airport and tell them I am traveling as a courier. Before I know it, I have got a crowd of twenty people surrounding me. But most important, be sure to tell them about this book so they too can save on airfare!

## WHAT ARE THE ADVANTAGES OF COURIER TRAVEL?

What is that saying, "You don't get something for nothing"? Well, in the case of courier travel, this is only partially true. While you do have the opportunity to save on airfares to nearly every major city around the world, there is a "price" to pay. But first let's look at the positive aspects.

The money you save is the greatest advantage to courier travel. How else can you fly from New York to Singapore for $150 roundtrip, or Los Angeles to London for $199? The money you save should more than compensate for any inconveniences that may arise. For those of you on a limited budget and who had planned on traveling light, this is a "win-win" situation.

There are no advance purchase penalties. When dealing with an airline directly, you often have to pay a hefty price for tickets not purchased seven, fourteen, or even twenty-one days in advance—a long time for you "spur of the moment" types. As an air courier, you will not be penalized for making travel arrangements only a few days in advance. In fact, your willingness to travel on the spur of the moment can be your leverage with the courier company. If the company needs to sell a ticket fast, you will probably be able to purchase the seat for very little or even free. For example, I recently found a courier flight from Los Angeles to Hong Kong for $150 roundtrip—provided I was willing to leave within three days. When I called the airline, I discovered that a ticket on that same flight and on that same date would cost over $1,500 if purchased through the "normal" route! That is ten times more than the cost of the courier flight. You do not have to be a brain surgeon to figure out what a terrific deal courier travel can be.

Finally, courier travel is fun. You will be exposed to a whole new industry and way of travel. When you meet another courier in the airport, you will have much to talk about—cities visited, courier companies used, and so forth. So when you meet that other courier in the airport, sit down, have a drink, and get to know your new friend.

## ARE THERE DISADVANTAGES?

There are a few limitations to courier travel; however, they are heavily outweighed by its advantages. The disadvantages begin with the fact that you will sometimes not be allowed to bring all of your luggage to be checked in (as the whole basis behind courier travel is that you give up some or all of your luggage space in return for a discounted ticket). Although this does not mean you must travel empty-handed. Most couriers are very creative people. (If they were not, they would be paying hundreds of dollars more for the same flight!) Use your creativity to get around this problem.

Even though you might not be able to check in luggage, you always will be allowed to bring one or two carry-on bags. The airlines usually do not bother you provided that you do not attempt to bring on a huge suitcase that you intend to fit under your seat. The airlines' flexibility with this rule is dependent on how full the flight is. Two full bags should be more than enough clothing to cover a week or two in a foreign city. Most people over-pack. I have yet to meet anybody who does not take too much, including myself. Traveling lightly is an advantage because it gives you greater mobility.

In the event you need more room, there is something else you can do. Though the airline will only allow two bags to be carried on, there is no restriction on the amount of clothing you can wear on the plane. I am very serious about this. If you need a heavy coat where you are going, wear it on the plane. Do the same for a heavy sweater, shirts, and so on.

You can always bring in your pocket a rolled-up nylon bag. Once on the plane, start shedding some of your clothing. The airline only restricts you on the number of bags that you can bring on the plane. If you board with two bags and disembark with three, consider yourself creative.

Another disadvantage to courier travel is the small hassle before and after your flight. Air courier companies usually require you to be at the airport one to three hours before the plane departs, depending on the destination. I actually enjoy this time because it has given me the opportunity to meet and talk with other couriers. Upon arrival you will also need to meet with a courier representative. Try not to let this small inconvenience sway you, though. It is small in comparison to the savings involved.

## How do I book a flight?

To book a flight, all you need is the information listed in this book. You do not need to be a member of any organization or association to be a courier. Be wary of those people who tell you otherwise. If you have any questions regarding this, feel free to write to me in care of the publisher.

While you need not be a member of any association, some courier companies charge you a minimal registration fee. For example, Now Voyager charges a $50 per year annual fee. This is noted in the courier company directory. My recommendation is to seek out courier companies first which do not have such a charge. Over the past couple of years, many of these charges have been eliminated.

Once you have decided on your destination, it is time to contact a courier company. You can skim through the directory of worldwide courier destinations to help you locate a city in which courier flights are available. The index in the back of this book will help you cross-reference destinations and departure cities. It is important to note that the cities to which companies offer courier flights are constantly changing. Once you have contacted the courier company, it will help you locate a date and a location that is available to them and acceptable to you.

If your goal is to take more than one courier flight on one trip, it is possible to arrange this through one company. Jupiter Air can do this. For example, if you want to fly from San Francisco to Singapore and then continue from Singapore to Bangkok, all of this can be arranged with one phone call. Or if you want to travel from Los Angeles to London and then from London to Tokyo, this is also possible by making only one phone call.

Another often asked question is, "how far in advance must a courier flight be booked?" Ideally, courier companies like to fill their schedules two to three months in advance. As an example of a two month schedule, beginning on October 1, the courier companies will take reservations for flights through December. Therefore, it is a good idea to contact companies on the first of the month, because that is when they open up their schedules. However, the best deals can be found if you are willing to travel on short notice.

At times, getting in contact with some courier companies is easier said than done. The phone lines at Now Voyager and Halbart Express are often tied up with other budget-minded travelers like yourself, and it may require a great deal of patience to get through. Some courier companies, such as World Courier, require you to call and leave your name and address, and they will mail you an application. This tends to be quite burdensome and is one reason why I have not flown with this company. Don't let these inconveniences deter you; it is still worth it. However, the majority of courier company offices are extremely friendly. They will assist you in getting you where you want to go for as inexpensively as possible. Some companies can offer you additional travel services, aside from the courier flights, such as non-courier flights.

Some courier companies, especially the larger ones, require you to call them a day before you make your reservation. These companies have extensive recorded messages detailing all the flights available, last minute bargains, length of stay, etc. This is important for these companies which offer so many courier flights, that it would take too long for them to explain everything to you. For example, one courier company offers over thirty roundtrip tickets between New York and London alone every week. They do not have the manpower to list all of these flights to callers personally. Some courier companies do not even handle the reservations themselves, opting instead to use courier brokers.

Not all courier companies are set up to book the flights, take reservations, handle payments, and deal with customers. This is where courier brokers fit in. The brokers essentially fill the seats for the courier companies. Courier brokers represent one or more courier companies. Therefore, they can provide you with numerous tickets on the same flight using different courier companies. However, nobody works for free. The courier broker usually adds a service fee to the price of the ticket. Generally, you will get a cheaper fare if you deal directly with the courier company. The advantage to courier brokers is they might represent many courier companies and have access to many more tickets or destinations. The directory will list whether the company is a broker or courier company.

After you make a reservation with a courier company—that is, after you initially call and choose a date and city—the company will send you a contract. Some companies require that you have the payment and the signed contract returned to them within a week. The generally accepted forms of payment will be discussed in the upcoming section. It is possible—and sometimes desirable—to have the courier company fax you a copy of the contract in order for you to get the payment to them more quickly and secure your reservation. Different courier companies have different requirements, formats, and policies.

It is important to keep track of your communications with the courier company, especially the name of the person you talked with. These people talk to many people each and every day and have a tendency to forget what was arranged with any particular person. Although the courier industry is quite large, the division of the courier company that schedules onboard couriers like yourself is usually quite small—often only one or two people. Additionally, when people call a courier company, they are expected to have a basic knowledge of courier travel. The courier company employees do not have the time to personally explain the basics of courier travel to every person that calls. This book does that for them.

## How can I pay for a courier flight?

Courier companies often have different ways of collecting payment: some accept credit cards while others accept only money orders or certified checks. Others will accept personal checks provided they have the opportunity to clear the bank prior to the flight's departure. Some companies can accept cash payments at their offices. So if you live in or near New York, Los Angeles, San Francisco, Toronto, or other cities that have courier flights departing from them, it is possible to pay in cash at the courier company office. This could be the case if you are flying at the last minute and do not have time to mail a check. For example, if you find a flight departing New York to Paris for $99 roundtrip that leaves in two days, you will have to make your payment in person at the courier office. Be sure to discuss this with them.

Most courier companies do not charge a deposit on the flight, although some courier companies still do. This is to ensure you take the roundtrip. This is especially true if you have never taken a courier flight with this particular company before. They do this to protect themselves from the possibility of somebody not fulfilling their end of the bargain. Deposits range from $50 to $500. Some companies allow you to put this deposit on a credit card while others require it up front. In this case, your deposit will be refunded upon your return. Sometimes, once you have flown with a company, the deposit is waived.

The important thing to remember about courier travel is that money talks. Usually, the first person to pay for a flight gets it. When a courier company pencils you in for a flight, it gives you a certain amount of time to get the payment in. For example, the company might give you five days, after which it will cancel your reservation and make the flight available to somebody else. Keep in touch with them. If you think your payment will not be received in time, call them to let them know this. You do not want to lose your flight due to miscommunication.

## How Long Can I Stay?

Length of stay is another subject with a lot of variables. In some cases, the courier company sets the length of stay. In others, the company sets a range of dates for return and you get to choose the length of your stay. Stays can range from one week to one year. When you look through the courier company directory, the lengths of stay will be listed in most cases. Whether they are listed or not, this is something you should discuss with the courier company. Most courier companies will work with your schedule. You are doing the courier company a favor. Without you, they would not be in business.

It is also possible to return from different cities. For example, one could fly to Mexico City and return from other cities in Mexico, such as Cancun or Acapulco. I've done this myself. Again, this depends on which courier company you choose to fly with. Be sure to ask them about this as well.

## Can I Cancel or Get a Refund?

If you must cancel a courier flight, cancellation charges generally do apply. The cancellation policy will be outlined in their contract. However in most cases, the percentage of your payment held depends on the number of days prior to the flight that the cancellation is made. If you cancel at the last minute, or miss your flight, you will probably lose the full amount of your fare. This policy is very similar to buying a non-refundable ticket on a commercial airline.

Refunds are usually not available; however, in certain cases I have heard of people receiving some refunds. This has to do with how far in advance they made their reservation and how far in advance they canceled their flight. Remember, the courier company must fill that seat on a certain day. When you see flights offered for free, they are sometimes the result of someone else's last-minute cancellation.

## CAN I TRAVEL WITH A COMPANION?

A bsolutely. While courier travel is extremely popular with the independent traveler, there are many opportunities for travel with a companion. While independent travel is enjoyable, and I have done a lot of it in my time, I prefer to share my international experiences with a partner. In my courier trips, I usually travel with my friend. While simple, courier travel with a companion does require some additional planning.

The basis of courier travel is to give up some or all of your luggage space in exchange for subsidized airfare. Therefore, a courier company might only need one seat on a particular flight. So if this is the case, how does your travel partner get there with you?

One method is to attempt to arrange for both of you to travel on the same flight with the same courier company. This is possible because some companies do send numerous couriers on the same flight. There are times when more than one courier is needed for heavy shipments. Courier brokers can assist you in getting two people on the same flight. This might be done through two different courier companies using the same broker. This is ideal because it only requires one phone call, and there is only one check to write.

Another possibility is for both of you to travel with the same courier company and on the same day, although on different flights. Some city combinations, such as from New York to London, are so popular that there is more than one courier flight per day. If you travel on different flights, then the first traveler may utilize the extra time by making arrangements for lodging.

One of the most common ways people travel together as couriers is for one person to travel one day and the other to fly the very next day. Remember that these companies purchase tickets for the same flight each and every day. For example, on a recent two-week courier trip to London, I flew on Tuesday and my friend flew on the same flight to London that Wednesday. When I originally tried to book our reservations, I asked for two consecutive days, preferably a Monday and Tuesday. Unfortunately, that Monday was already booked, so we took the Tuesday and Wednesday courier flights. Flexibility is paramount with courier travel. This is how you will save the greatest amount of money.

Upon my arrival, I used the extra day to locate an inexpensive place to stay in London—not an easy task, I might say. Check the resource section in this book for a list of budget accommodations in major courier cities. Whatever slight inconvenience I encountered, it was more than made up for by the money we saved. Additionally, the courier company allowed my wife and me to switch the return dates in order for my wife to return to the States the day before I did. Most courier companies will attempt to work with you. If you have a specific travel request, be sure to ask the courier company.

Flying to different cities and then meeting later is another possibility for people traveling together. For example, one person could fly to Singapore and the other to Bangkok. Or, one person could fly to Madrid and the other to Lisbon. Transportation between the cities is relatively inexpensive. This is usually very easy to arrange, because most courier companies offer flights to major cities each and every day.

Yet another option is for one person to fly using a commercial ticket on the same flight as the courier. Although one ticket will cost substantially more, the two of you can split the cost and you will still be flying for less than anyone else on that airplane. For example, you could buy a ticket through a courier company to Hong Kong for $200 roundtrip. Your travel partner could buy a ticket on the same flight for $800 roundtrip through a travel agent. The total cost to both of you would be $1,000 or $500 each, far less than any other way to Hong Kong, except perhaps by the proverbial slow boat to China. The choice is yours.

Although you must be at least eighteen to fly as a courier, it is still possible to travel with children. Many courier companies allow you to bring a child without any additional charge. There are usually some restrictions. For instance, one company might allow you to bring a child provided they are over the age of two, while another company might have a different requirement. One thing is for sure, you will not be allowed to take any nineteen-year-old children with you for free. An additional restriction will be based on the airline's rules regarding children. For example, some airlines allow children to fly for free only up until the age of two, whereas other airlines might have different policies.

## What are my responsibilities as a courier?

Your most important responsibility is to follow the requirements designated by the courier company. These requirements will be outlined in your contract, which you usually must sign. Some courier companies also have a "Terms and Conditions" sheet, which they will make you aware of.

First and foremost, you are not an employee of the courier company. You are an independent contractor. You are not on their payroll, they will not pay your health insurance, and you will not receive a pension. What you will receive is a deeply discounted airline ticket.

However, you will be representing the courier company both to the public and to the airline, even if nobody knows you are a courier. You can be sure that if you get drunk on your flight and are arrested, the courier company will hear about it. Do not jeopardize courier travel for the rest of us. You have a responsibility to your fellow travelers to not destroy this tradition.

Different courier companies have different expectations of your conduct. Some courier companies will not allow you to drink alcohol; others will. That does not mean if you are flying as a courier on British Airways, which offers complimentary alcoholic beverages, that you should finish off every drink on the plane. The bottom line is: know your limits.

## THE DAY OF THE FLIGHT

The day of the flight you will need to meet an agent from the courier company at a place designated by the company. This can be at any one of a number of locations, including a specific spot at the airport terminal or at the courier company office, usually located on the grounds of the airport. The airport terminal is the most common location.

The courier company will usually require you to be at the airport a minimum of two hours prior to the flight in order for them to check your passport, check in any luggage you might have, give you a copy of the manifest and check you in for the flight. Additionally, the agent you meet prior to flight will give you a printed copy of instructions, which includes your return flight information and where to meet the courier agent when you arrive. Usually, this process does not take long. The courier representatives are very helpful—remember, you are actually doing them a great favor. Without you, they would not be in business.

You will not be required to do any lifting, lugging, carrying, tugging, dragging, pushing, pulling, or hauling of any material for a courier company. You are essentially just going along for the ride. The courier company delivers the material to the airline and picks it up upon arrival. Your job is merely to show the manifest to the customs officer when you reach your destination.

Courier companies have different requirements concerning dress. Many require you to dress professionally whereas others will let you fly in shorts. This is another question you need to discuss with the courier company. You should not have any problems if your appearance is not in the extreme.

Yet another responsibility has to do with flight confirmation. Often you need to call the courier company to confirm your flight schedule. This is done to ensure that you know when you are traveling. They might ask you to confirm this on both the departure and return flights.

You will need a valid passport, which will enable entry to and exit from your courier destination. Furthermore, you might need a visa, depending on where you are traveling to. You are responsible for all your own lodging and all your other expenses when you reach your destination. Some flights do include stopovers in various cities, and in these cases the courier companies will pay for your night's lodging in these cities.

Now you have the information you need to travel inexpensively and enjoy many exciting destinations. The following page includes a list of courier tips to ensure your trip goes as smoothly as possible. The resource section will assist you with lodging and travel information. I hope courier travel brings you as much enjoyment as it has for me over the years. Good luck and happy travels!

# COURIER TIPS

✈ Be aware of the basics of supply and demand. Seek out off-season travel for the best savings.

✈ Call courier companies at the beginning of the month for the best selection of available flights.

✈ Ensure that you have a visa if one is required, and keep your passport up to date.

✈ Carry *The Courier Air Travel Handbook* with you when you travel, which details the phone numbers of worldwide courier companies for easy reference.

✈ Join the frequent flyer program of the airline.

✈ When meeting the courier company, be sure you have change with you for a phone call in case they are late or you are in the wrong place.

✈ Pack lightly. Just about everybody over-packs. The less stuff you have, the more mobile you will be.

✈ Try to plan ahead and have an idea of where you will stay the first night.

✈ Keep your passport, return ticket, courier information, and traveler's checks in a safe place. Losing one of these items can be painful.

✈ Remember that each courier company has its own set of policies, and you must follow their procedures exactly.

# PART II

# Courier

# Company Directory

The following pages list active courier companies. Please note the proper times to call; this will save you time and money. Although phone numbers do change, at the time of printing all numbers were current. Every attempt has been made to locate toll-free numbers; however, these numbers are often closely-guarded secrets.

The directory is organized by geographic region and then by country. Courier companies are listed alphabetically under the cities in which their flights originate.

# Courier Directory Contents

## NORTH AMERICA

# CENTRAL AND SOUTH AMERICA

# PACIFIC RIM

# EUROPE

# NORTH AMERICA

**COURIER COMPANY LISTINGS**

# UNITED STATES

## CHICAGO

### Halbart Express

| Destination | Round trip/last minute fare | Length of stay/Departure days |
|---|---|---|
| **London** | **$450/$300** | **Up to 2 months; Wed–Mon** |

**Flights originating from:** Chicago
**Address:** 1475 Elmhurst Road, Elk Grove Village, IL 60007
**Phone:** (847) 806-1250
**Toll-free number:** No
**Point of contact:** Cherise
**Times to call:** 1PM–3PM CST Mon–Fri
**Recorded information:** No
**Type of business:** Courier
**Conducting business since:** 1983
**Annual registration fee:** No
**Courier assignment length:** Up to 30 days
**Luggage restrictions:** Carry-on only
**Frequest flyer mileage accrued:** Yes
**Airlines used:** American
**Return date flexibility:** Yes
**One-way tickets available:** No
**Cancellation phone list:** Yes
**Last-minute discounts:** Yes
**Additional non-courier travel services:** No
**Recommended advance reservations:** 4 to 6 weeks
**Earliest possible reservations:** 1 to 2 months
**Departure taxes:** No
**Deposit:** $100 deposit for Monday and Thursday departures
**Method of payment:** Money order; certified check
**Credit cards accepted:** No
**Comments:** The staff are very friendly and helpful. This company began service to Hong Kong in March 1998, but there was insufficient information at press time to add a listing.

## Jupiter/Micom America

| Destination | Round trip/last-minute fare | Length of stay/Departure days |
|---|---|---|
| **Hong Kong** | **$550/Varies** | **7–30 days; Tue–Sun** |

**Flights originating from:** Chicago
**Address:** 220 Howard Avenue, Des Plains, IL 60018
**Phone:** (847) 298-3850
**Fax:** (847) 298-3854
**Toll-free number:** No
**Point of contact:** Eiba
**Times to call:** 9AM–5PM CST Mon–Fri
**Recorded information:** No
**Type of business:** Courier
**Conducting business since:** 1988
**Annual registration fee:** $35
**Courier assignment length:** 7 to 30 days
**Luggage restrictions:** Carry-on only
**Frequent flyer mileage accrued:** Yes
**Airlines used:** JAL
**Return date flexibility:** No
**One-way tickets available:** Yes
**Cancellation phone list:** Yes
**Last-minute discounts:** Yes
**Additional non-courier travel services:** No
**Recommended advance reservations:** 1 month
**Earliest possible reservations:** 1 month
**Departure taxes:** Yes
**Deposit:** $100
**Method of payment:** Money order; certified check
**Credit cards accepted:** No
**Comments:** If you want to ensure a return date that works with your schedule, you should call one month before departure.

# Travel Headquarters

| Destination | Round trip/last-minute fare | Length of stay/Departure days |
|---|---|---|
| **Hong Kong** | **$500–$600/Varies** | **7–30 days; 5 days a week** |
| **London** | **$350–$500/Varies** | **7–30 days; 4 days a week** |

**Flights originating from:** Chicago
**Address:** 59 Eisenhower Lane, Lombard, IL 60148
**Phone:** (630) 620-8080
**Fax:** (630) 620-8147
**Toll-free number:** No
**Point of contact:** Norm
**Times to call:** 9AM–5PM CST Mon–Fri
**Recorded information:** No
**Type of business:** Booking Agent
**Annual registration fee:** No
**Courier assignment length:** 7 to 30 days
**Luggage restrictions:** Carry-on only to London; Carry-on and one checked bag to Hong Kong
**Frequent flyer mileage accrued:** Varies
**Airlines used:** American, JAL
**Return date flexibility:** Yes
**One-way tickets available:** No
**Cancellation phone list:** Yes
**Last-minute discounts:** Yes
**Additional non-courier travel services:** Yes
**Recommended advance reservations:** 2 months
**Earliest possible reservations:** 90 days
**Departure taxes:** No
**Deposit:** $100
**Method of payment:** Money order; certified check; cash
**Credit cards accepted:** No
**Comments:** Last-minute fares are available on a very limited basis.

# LOS ANGELES

## East–West Express

| Destination | Round trip/last-minute fare | Length of stay/Departure days |
|---|---|---|
| Aukland | $1,225/No | Up to 30 days; flights daily |
| Brisbane | $1,225/No | Up to 90 days; flights daily |
| Cairns | $1,225/No | Up to 90 days; flights daily |
| Melbourne | $1,225/No | Up to 90 days; flights daily |
| Sydney | $1,225/No | Up to 90 days; flights daily |

**Flights originating from:** Los Angeles
Address: P.O. Box 30849, JFK Airport Station, Jamaica, NY 11430
**Phone:** (718) 656-6246
**Fax:** (718) 656-6247
**Toll-free number:** No
**Point of contact:** Tracy
**Times to call:** 9AM–5PM EST
**Recorded information:** No
**Type of business:** Courier Broker
**Conducting business since:** 1991
**Annual registration fee:** No
**Courier assignment length:** Up to 90 days
**Luggage restrictions:** Carry-on only on the outgoing flight. You can check bags on the return flight.
**Frequent flyer mileage accrued:** No
**Airlines used:** Qantas
**Return date flexibility:** Yes
**One-way tickets available:** No
**Cancellation phone list:** No
**Last-minute discounts:** No
**Additional non-courier travel services:** No
**Recommended advance reservations:** 2 months
**Earliest possible reservations:** 2 months
**Departure taxes:** No
**Deposit:** No
**Method of payment:** Certified check; cash
**Credit cards accepted:** No
**Comments:** This company is friendly and helpful. The Australia trips are popular, so you will definitely need to book in advance.

# Film International

| Destination | Round trip/last-minute fare | Length of stay/Departure days |
|---|---|---|
| **Mexico City** | **$275/Varies** | **Up to 1 month; Mon–Thu, Sat** |

**Flights originating from:** Los Angeles
**Address:** 8900 Bellance Avenue, Los Angeles, CA 90045
**Phone:** (310) 568-8403
**Toll-free number:** No
**Point of contact:** Milton
**Times to call:** 9AM–5PM PST
**Recorded information:** No
**Type of business:** Courier Broker
**Conducting business since:** 1984
**Annual registration fee:** No
**Courier assignment length:** Up to 1 month
**Luggage restrictions:** Carry-on only; checked bags are an additional $31, space permitting.
**Frequent flyer mileage accrued:** Yes
**Airlines used:** Lacsa
**Return date flexibility:** Yes
**One-way tickets available:** No
**Cancellation phone list:** Yes
**Last-minute discounts:** Yes
**Additional non-courier travel services:** No
**Recommended advance reservations:** 1 month
**Earliest possible reservations:** 1 month
**Departure taxes:** No
**Deposit**: $100 non-refundable
**Method of payment:** Personal check; cash
**Credit cards accepted:** No
**Comments:** These flights are irregular. Please call to find out when flights depart.

## Halbart Express

| Destination | Round trip/last-minute fare | Length of stay/Departure days |
|---|---|---|
| **London** | **$350-$400/No** | **7–21 days; Tue–Thu, Sat** |
| **Manila** | **$400/No** | **14–90 days; Tue–Thu, Sat** |
| **Syndey** | **$750/No** | **2 weeks; Tue, Wed, Sat** |

**Flights originating from:** Los Angeles
**Address:** 1000 West Hillcrest Boulevard, Inglewood, CA 90301
**Phone:** (310) 417-3048
**Fax:** (310) 417-9729
**Toll-free number:** No
**Point of contact:** Anyone
**Times to call:** 9AM–3PM EST Mon–Fri
**Recorded information:** Yes
**Type of business:** Courier Company
**Conducting business since:** 1983
**Annual registration fee:** No
**Courier assignment length:** 2 weeks
**Luggage restrictions:** Varies by flight; some are carry-on only.
**Frequent flyer mileage accrued:** Varies by flight; ask when booking.
**Airlines used:** Air New Zealand, Northwest, TWA, American
**Return date flexibility:** No
**One-way tickets available:** Rarely
**Cancellation phone list:** Yes
**Last-minute discounts:** Yes
**Additional non-courier travel services:** No
**Recommended advance reservations:** 2 months
**Earliest possible reservations:** 2 to 3 months
**Departure taxes:** No
**Deposit:** $100 deposit
**Method of payment:** Certified check; money order
**Credit cards accepted:** No
**Comments:** These flights fill up fast. You'll need to call a couple of months in advance.

# International Bonded Couriers (IBC)

| Destination | Round trip/last-minute fare | Length of stay/Departure days |
|---|---|---|
| **Bangkok** | **$450/$200** | **2 weeks; Mon–Fri** |
| **Hong Kong** | **$350/$150** | **2 weeks; Tue–Sat** |
| **Manila** | **$350/$250** | **2 weeks; Tue–Sat** |
| **Seoul** | **$400/Varies** | **1–2 weeks; Fri only** |
| **Singapore** | **$350/$150** | **Up to 2 months; Tue–Sat** |

**Flights originating from:** Los Angeles
**Address:** 5793 West Imperial Highway; Los Angeles International Airport, Los Angeles, CA 90045
**Phone:** (310) 665-1760
**Fax:** (310) 665-0247
**Toll-free number:** No
**Point of contact:** Yolanda
**Times to call:** 9AM–4PM PST Tue–Fri
**Recorded information:** Yes
**Type of business:** Courier Company
**Conducting business since:** 1988
**Annual registration fee:** No
**Courier assignment length:** 1 to 3 weeks
**Luggage restrictions:** Carry-on only
**Frequent flyer mileage accrued:** No
**Airlines used:** Northwest, Singapore, United
**Return date flexibility:** No
**One-way tickets available:** No
**Cancellation phone list:** Yes
**Last-minute discounts:** No
**Additional non-courier travel services:** Yes
**Recommended advance reservations:** 4 to 6 weeks
**Earliest possible reservations:** 4 to 6 weeks
**Departure taxes:** No
**Deposit:** $500
**Method of payment:** Certified check; money order; personal check; cash
**Credit cards accepted:** Yes
**Comments:** Prices usually remain the same throughout the year.

## Johnny Air Cargo

| Destination | Round trip/last-minute fare | Length of stay/Departure days |
|---|---|---|
| **Manila** | **$450–$850/No** | **Up to 3 months; 3–4 days/wk** |

**Flights originating from:** Los Angeles
**Address:** 203 South Vermont Avenue, Los Angeles, CA 90004
**Phone:** (213) 386-7080
**Fax:** (213) 386-7277
**Toll-free number:** 800-991-7080
**Point of contact:** Lisa Locsin
**Times to call:** 11AM–6PM PST Mon–Fri
**Recorded information:** No
**Type of business:** Courier
**Annual registration fee:** No
**Courier assignment length:** Up to 3 months
**Luggage restrictions:** Carry-on and 1 checked bag
**Frequent flyer mileage accrued:** Varies
**Airlines used:** Korean Airlines, China Airlines
**Return date flexibility:** Yes
**One-way tickets available:** No
**Cancellation phone list:** No
**Last-minute discounts:** No
**Additional non-courier travel services:** Yes
**Recommended advance reservations:** 1 month
**Earliest possible reservations:** 1 month
**Departure taxes:** No
**Deposit:** Varies
**Method of payment:** Personal check; cash
**Credit cards accepted:** No

## Jupiter Air

| Destination | Round trip/last-minute fare | Length of stay/Departure days |
|---|---|---|
| **Hong Kong** | **$450/Varies** | **Up to 1 month; flights daily** |
| **Bangkok** | **$450/Varies** | **Up to 1 month; flights daily** |
| **Seoul** | **$350/Varies** | **Up to 1 month; flights daily** |
| **Singapore** | **$450/Varies** | **Up to 1 month; flights daily** |

**Flights originating from:** Los Angeles
**Address:** 460 South Hindry Avenue, Unit D, Inglewood, CA 90301
**Phone:** (310) 670-1197 or (310) 670-1198
**Fax:** (310) 649-2771
**Toll-free number:** No
**Point of contact:** Grace or Melissa
**Times to call:** 9AM–5:30PM PST Mon–Fri
**Recorded information:** No
**Type of business:** Courier Company
**Conducting business since:** 1988
**Annual registration fee:** $35
**Courier assignment length:** Up to 1 month
**Luggage restrictions:** 1 carry-on and 1 checked bag
**Frequent flyer mileage accrued:** No
**Airlines used:** JAL, Singapore, Asiana
**Return date flexibility:** Varies
**One-way tickets available:** No
**Cancellation phone list:** No
**Last-minute discounts:** Yes
**Additional non-courier travel services:** No
**Recommended advance reservations:** 2 months
**Earliest possible reservations:** 2 months
**Departure taxes:** No
**Deposit:** $100
**Method of payment:** Money order
**Credit cards accepted:** No
**Comments:** Prices are slightly higher during summer months.

## Now Voyager

| Destination | Round trip/last-minute fare | Length of stay/Departure days |
|---|---|---|
| **Aukland** | **$730–$900/Varies** | **Up to 30 days; Sat** |
| **Sydney** | **$699–$1,199/Varies** | **Variable flight dates** |

**Flights originating from:** Los Angeles
**Address:** 74 Varick Street, Suite 307, New York, NY 10013
**Phone:** (212) 431-1616
**Fax:** (212) 219-1753 or (212) 334-5243
**Toll-free number:** No
**Point of contact:** Anyone
**Times to call:** 10AM–5:30PM EST Mon–Fri
**Recorded information:** 11PM–5:30PM EST Mon–Fri
**Type of business:** Courier Broker
**Conducting business since:** 1983
**Annual registration fee:** $50
**Courier assignment length:** Up to 3 months
**Luggage restrictions:** Carry-on only
**Frequent flyer mileage accrued:** Yes
**Airlines used:** Qantas, Air New Zealand
**Return date flexibility:** No
**One-way tickets available:** No
**Cancellation phone list:** Yes
**Last-minute discounts:** Yes
**Additional non-courier travel services:** Yes
**Recommended advance reservations:** 2 to 3 months
**Earliest possible reservations:** 2 to 3 months
**Departure taxes:** No
**Deposit:** $100
**Method of payment:** Money order; certified check; cash
**Credit cards accepted:** Yes
**Comments:** This is a busy company and it is difficult to get through by phone.
First-time flyers should listen to the recording. All flights must be booked from the
New York office. Also offers continuing flights to Melbourne, Brisbane, and Cairns.

# Virgin Wholesale Express

| Destination | Round trip/last-minute fare | Length of stay/Departure days |
|---|---|---|
| **London** | **$460/No** | **Up to 6 weeks** |

**Flights originating from:** Los Angeles
**Address:** Building 197, JFK International Airport, Jamaica, NY 11430
**Phone:** (718) 529-6814
**Fax:** (718) 529-6817
**Toll-free number:** No
**Point of contact:** Janet or Leslie
**Times to call:** 10AM–5PM EST Mon–Fri
**Recorded information:** No
**Type of business:** Courier Broker
**Conducting business since:** 1991
**Annual registration fee:** No
**Courier assignment length:** Up to 6 weeks
**Luggage restrictions:** Carry-on and 2 checked bags
**Frequent flyer mileage accrued:** Yes
**Airlines used:** Virgin Atlantic
**Return date flexibility:** No
**One-way tickets available:** No
**Cancellation phone list:** No
**Last-minute discounts:** No
**Additional non-courier travel services:** No
**Recommended advance reservations:** 2 months
**Earliest possible reservations:** 2 months
**Departure taxes:** Included in price
**Deposit:** No
**Method of payment:** Money order; certified check; personal check
**Credit cards accepted:** Yes
**Comments:** For cancellations between one and thirty days before the flight, only a 10% refund is given; for cancellations more than thirty days before the flight, 50% of the price is refunded.

# MIAMI

## Halbart Express

| Destination | Round trip/last-minute fare | Length of stay/Departure days |
|---|---|---|
| Sao Paulo* | $400/Varies | 1 week; Mon–Sat |
| London | $475/Varies | 7 days; Mon–Sat |
| Rio de Janiero | $350/Varies | 7-30 days; Mon, Tue, Thu, Fri |

*Flights to Sao Paulo were temporarily suspended during early 1998.

**Flights originating from:** Miami
**Address:** 7331 Northwest 72nd Avenue, Miami, FL 33122
**Phone:** (305) 593-0260
**Fax:** (305) 593-0158
**Toll-free number:** No
**Point of contact:** Joe
**Times to call:** 9AM–5PM EST Mon–Fri
**Recorded information:** No
**Type of business:** Courier Company
**Conducting business since:** 1983
**Annual registration fee:** No
**Courier assignment length:** 1 week
**Luggage restrictions:** Carry-on only
**Frequent flyer mileage accrued:** Yes
**Airlines used:** American, Varig
**Return date flexibility:** No
**One-way tickets available:** No
**Cancellation phone list:** Yes
**Last-minute discounts:** Rarely
**Additional non-courier travel services:** No
**Recommended advance reservations:** 2 to 3 weeks
**Earliest possible reservations:** 2 to 3 weeks
**Departure taxes:** No
**Deposit:** No
**Method of payment:** Certified check; money order
**Credit cards accepted:** No
**Comments:** Prices are slightly higher during summer months. The Miami office of Halbart is extremely friendly and helpful. I highly recommend this company for courier flights. They offer good opportunities for heavily discounted, and sometimes free, flights. On one day in August 1993, Halbart gave a round-trip ticket to Santiago for free, to Buenos Aires for $178, and to Caracas for $99!

# International Bonded Couriers (IBC)

| Destination | Round trip/last-minute fare | Length of stay/Departure days |
|---|---|---|
| **Buenos Aires** | **$450-$800/No** | **Up to 30 days; Mon–Thu, Sat** |
| **Caracas** | **$300/No** | **7 days; Mon–Thu, Sat** |
| **Guatemala** | **$349/No** | **7 days; Mon–Thu, Sat** |
| **Jamaica** | **$249/No** | **7 days; Mon–Thu, Sat** |
| **Santiago** | **$699/No** | **7 days; Mon–Thu, Sat** |

**Flights originating from:** Miami
**Address:** 8401 NW 17th Street, Miami, FL 33126
**Phone:** (305) 597-5331
**Fax:** (305) 591-2056
**Toll-free number:** No
**Point of contact:** Carolina
**Times to call:** 7AM–3PM EST
**Recorded information:** No
**Type of business:** Courier Broker
**Conducting business since:** 1981
**Annual registration fee:** No
**Courier assignment length:** Up to 30 days
**Luggage restrictions:** 1 carry-on only
**Frequent flyer mileage accrued:** No
**Airlines used:** Aerolinas Argentina, Lan Chile, Air Jamaica
**Return date flexibility:** Yes
**One-way tickets available:** No
**Cancellation phone list:** Yes
**Last-minute discounts:** No
**Additional non-courier travel services:** No
**Recommended advance reservations:** 1 month
**Earliest possible reservations:** 1 month
**Departure taxes:** Included in price
**Deposit:** No
**Method of payment:** Money order; certified check; cash
**Credit cards accepted:** No

On some courier flights, you will only be allowed to have carry-on bags. Your luggage space is used to transport packages for the courier company. Sometimes, however, you will be able to check luggage as well as bring carry-on bags.

## Lima Services

| Destination | Round trip/last-minute fare | Length of stay/Departure days |
|---|---|---|
| **Lima** | **$250–$430/Varies** | **Up to 30 days; flights daily** |

**Flights originating from:** Miami
**Address:** 6115 Johnson Street, Hollywood, FL 33024
**Phone:** (954) 964-8400
**Fax:** (954) 964-0700
**Toll-free number:** No
**Point of contact:** Elva or Gladys
**Recorded information:** No
**Type of business:** Courier company
**Annual registration fee:** No
**Courier assignment length:** Up to 30 days
**Airlines used:** AeroPeru
**Comments:** Call and ask to be placed on their list. They will call you when a flight becomes available.

# Linehaul Services

| Destination | Round trip/last-minute fare | Length of stay/Departure days |
|---|---|---|
| **Buenos Aires** | **$473/Varies** | **5–30 days; Mon–Thu, Sat** |
| **Caracas** | **$173/Varies** | **5–30 days; Mon–Thu, Sat** |
| **Guatemala City** | **$273/Varies** | **5–30 days; Mon–Thu, Sat** |
| **La Paz** | **$278/Varies** | **5–30 days; Mon–Thu, Sat** |
| **Lima** | **$250/Varies** | **5–30 days; Mon–Thu, Sat** |
| **Managua** | **$223/Varies** | **5–30 days; Mon–Thu, Sat** |
| **Panama City** | **$230/Varies** | **5–30 days; Mon–Thu, Sat** |
| **Quito** | **$236/Varies** | **5–30 days; Mon–Thu, Sat** |
| **Rio de Janeiro** | **$350–$500/Varies** | **5–30 days; Mon–Thu, Sat** |
| **Sao Paulo** | **$350–500/Varies** | **5–30 days; Mon–Thu, Sat** |

**Flights originating from:** Miami
**Address:** 7200 NW 19th Street, Miami, FL 33126
**Phone:** (305) 477-0651
**Fax:** (305) 477-0659
**Toll-free number:** No
**Point of contact:** Jackie
**Times to call:** 9AM–5:30PM Mon–Fri; 10:30AM–1:30PM Sat EST
**Recorded information:** No
**Type of business:** Courier Company
**Conducting business since:** 1985
**Annual registration fee:** No
**Courier assignment length:** 5 to 30 days
**Luggage restrictions:** Carry-on only
**Frequent flyer mileage accrued:** Yes
**Airlines used:** American, Argentina, Trans Brazil, Boliviano
**Return date flexibility:** Yes
**One-way tickets available:** Yes
**Cancellation phone list:** Yes
**Last-minute discounts:** Yes
**Additional non-courier travel services:** Yes
**Recommended advance reservations:** 45 days to 2 months
**Earliest possible reservations:** Can reserve up to 1 year in advance
**Departure taxes:** Included in price
**Deposit:** $200 for Sao Paulo and Rio de Janeiro
**Method of payment:** Money order; cash
**Credit cards accepted:** No
**Comments:** Prices are slightly higher during summer months. This company is very helpful. They speak Spanish. To qualify for last-minute fares you must live in Miami.

## Trans-Air System

| Destination | Round trip/last-minute fare | Length of stay/Departure days |
|---|---|---|
| **Guatemala City** | **$280/Varies** | **30 days; Mon–Fri** |
| **Quito** | **$250/Varies** | **30 days; Sun–Thu** |

**Flights originating from:** Miami
**Address:** 7264 NW 25th Street, Miami, FL 33122
**Phone:** (305) 592-1771
**Fax:** (305) 592-2927
**Toll-free number:** No
**Point of contact:** Gloria
**Times to call:** 9:30AM–5:30PM EST Mon–Fri
**Recorded information:** No
**Type of business:** Courier Company
**Conducting business since:** 1988
**Annual registration fee:** No
**Courier assignment length:** 1 week to 1 year
**Luggage restrictions:** Carry-on only
**Frequent flyer mileage accrued:** Yes
**Airlines used:** American
**Return date flexibility:** Yes
**One-way tickets available:** Yes
**Cancellation phone list:** Yes
**Last-minute discounts:** Yes
**Additional non-courier travel services:** No
**Recommended advance reservations:** 1 month
**Earliest possible reservations:** 2 months
**Departure taxes:** $28
**Deposit:** $50
**Method of payment:** Money order; cash
**Credit cards accepted:** No
**Comments:** Prices are slightly higher during summer months. This company is very helpful. They speak Spanish. Return date flexibility is limited.

# NEW YORK

## Air Facility

| Destination | Round trip/last-minute fare | Length of stay/Departure days |
|---|---|---|
| **Buenos Aires** | **$470/None** | **7–15 days; Mon–Thu, Sat** |
| **Caracas** | **$210/None** | **7–14 days; Mon–Thu, Sat** |
| **Montevideo** | **$480/None** | **7–15 days; Mon–Thu, Sat** |
| **Rio de Janiero** | **$405/$300** | **7–14 days; Mon–Thu, Sun** |
| **Santiago** | **$460/None** | **8–9 days; Mon–Thu, Sat** |
| **Sao Paulo** | **$395/$300** | **6–13 days; Mon–Thu, Sat** |

**Flights originating from:** New York
**Address:** 153-40 Rockaway Boulevard, Jamaica, NY 11434
**Phone:** (718) 712-1769
**Fax:** (718) 712-2597
**Toll-free number:** No
**Point of contact:** Marisa
**Times to call:** 9AM–4:30PM EST Mon–Fri
**Recorded information:** No
**Type of business:** Courier Company
**Conducting business since:** 1988
**Annual registration fee:** No
**Courier assignment length:** 1 to 2 weeks
**Luggage restrictions:** Carry-on only
**Frequent flyer mileage accrued:** Yes
**Airlines used:** Varig, United
**Return date flexibility:** No
**One-way tickets available:** No
**Cancellation phone list:** Yes
**Last-minute discounts:** Yes
**Additional non-courier travel services:** No
**Recommended advance reservations:** 2 months
**Earliest possible reservations:** 2 months
**Departure taxes:** $40 in cash
**Deposit:** No
**Method of payment:** Certified check; money order; cash
**Credit cards accepted:** No
**Comments:** Prices are slightly higher during summer months and in December. Air Facility depends on responsible people to act as couriers for them. If you cancel a flight last minute, they place you on a black list, and you will not be allowed to fly with them in the future. They are helpful and offer consistently inexpensive fares to South America.

## Air-Tech Ltd.

| Destination | Round trip/last-minute fare | Length of stay/Departure days |
|---|---|---|
| Bangkok | $600–$700/Varies | Up to 90 days |
| Buenos Aires | $550/Varies | Up to 2 weeks |
| Caracas | $250/Varies | Up to 2 weeks |
| Copenhagen | $200/Varies | Up to 1 week; Mon–Thu, Sat |
| Dublin | $289–$320/Varies | Up to 1 week; Mon–Thu, Sat |
| Hong Kong | $300–$650/Varies | Up to 3 months; Mon–Fri |
| Johannesburg | $1,000/Varies | Up to 45 days |
| London | $275–$375/Varies | Up to 1 month; Mon–Fri, Sun |
| Manila | $700–$800/Varies | Up to 3 months |
| Milan | $289–$450/Varies | 1–2 weeks; Mon–Sat |
| Montevideo | $550/Varies | 1 week; Mon–Thu, Sat–Sun |
| Paris | $300–$350/Varies | 1 week; Mon–Thu, Sat–Sun |
| Rio de Janiero | $550/Varies | Up to 2 weeks |
| Rome | $289–$450/Varies | 1–2 weeks; Mon–Thu, Sat |
| Santiago | $550/Varies | Up to 9 days |
| Sao Paulo | $550/Varies | Up to 2 weeks |
| Seoul | $700–$800/Varies | Up to 3 months |
| Singapore | $500–$600/Varies | Up to 3 months; Mon–Fri |
| Taipei | $650–$800/Varies | Up to 3 months |
| Tokyo | $600–$700/Varies | Up to 3 months |

**Flights originating from:** New York
**Address:** 588 Broadway, Suite 204, New York, NY 10012
**Phone:** (212) 219-7000
**Fax:** (212) 219-0066
**Point of contact:** Rita
**Times to call:** 9AM–5PM EST
**Recorded information:** No
**Type of business:** Courier Broker
**Courier assignment length:** Varies
**Luggage restrictions:** Carry-on only
**Frequent flyer mileage accrued:** Varies
**Airlines used:** United, South African, Lanchile, KLM, American, Aer Lingus, Japan, Aeromex, TWA, Varig
**Return date flexibility:** Yes
**One-way tickets available:** Yes
**Cancellation phone list:** No
**Last-minute discounts:** Yes
**Additional non-courier travel services:** Yes
**Recommended advance reservations:** 2 months
**Earliest possible reservations:** 3 months
**Departure taxes:** Yes
**Deposit:** Varies
**Method of payment:** Money order; certified check; personal check; cash
**Credit cards accepted:** Yes
**Comments:** Flights also available from Los Angeles, San Francisco, Chicago, and Miami. Call the New York office for flight information.

## All Nations Express

| Destination | Round trip/last-minute fare | Length of stay/Departure days |
| --- | --- | --- |
| **Seoul** | **$670/No** | **No limit; Tue–Thu, Sat** |

**Flights originating from:** New York
**Address:** 149-35 177th Street, Room 103, Jamaica, NY 11434
**Phone:** (718) 553-1718
**Fax:** (718) 553-1720
**Toll-free number:** No
**Point of contact:** Mr. Lee Chang Yeoul
**Times to call:** 9AM–5PM EST Mon–Fri
**Recorded information:** No
**Type of business:** Courier
**Annual registration fee:** No
**Courier assignment length:** Unlimited
**Luggage restrictions:** 1 carry-on and 1 checked bag
**Frequent flyer mileage accrued:** Yes
**Airlines used:** Asiana
**Return date flexibility:** Yes
**One-way tickets available:** No
**Cancellation phone list:** No
**Last-minute discounts:** No
**Additional non-courier travel services:** No
**Recommended advance reservations:** 1 month
**Earliest possible reservations:** 1 month
**Departure taxes:** No
**Deposit:** No
**Method of payment:** Money order; certified check; cash
**Credit cards accepted:** Yes
**Comments:** Very limited availability

## Courier Network

| Destination | Round trip/last-minute fare | Length of stay/Departure days |
|---|---|---|
| **Tel Aviv** | **$500–$700/None** | **7–45 days; Mon–Sat** |

**Flights originating from:** New York
**Address:** 515 West 29th Street, New York, NY 10001
**Phone:** (212) 947-3738
Toll-free number: (800) 222-9951
**Point of contact:** Yossi
**Times to call:** 6:30PM–8:30PM EST
**Recorded information:** No
**Type of business:** Courier Broker
**Conducting business since:** 1987
**Annual registration fee:** No
**Courier assignment length:** 2 months
**Luggage restrictions:** 1 carry-on and 1 checked bag
**Frequent flyer mileage accrued:** Yes
**Airlines used:** Major
**Return date flexibility:** Yes
**One-way tickets available:** No
**Cancellation phone list:** No
**Last-minute discounts:** No
**Additional non-courier travel services:** Yes
**Recommended advance reservations:** 2 months
**Earliest possible reservations:** 2 months
**Departure taxes:** No
**Deposit:** No
**Method of payment:** Personal check; cash
**Credit cards accepted:** Yes
**Comments:** I found this company to be neither friendly nor helpful. I recommend using another company, if possible. If you do decide to call, you may need to be persistent in order to get the information you need.

# Discount Travel International (DTI)

| Destination | Round trip/last-minute fare | Length of stay/Departure days |
|---|---|---|
| Amsterdam | $299–$399/Varies | Up to 30 days; Tue–Sat |
| Athens | $199–$499/Varies | Up to 30 days; Mon–Sat |
| Auckland | $699–$999/Varies | Up to 3 months; Wed, Sat |
| Bali | $599–$799/Varies | Up to 3 months; Mon–Sat |
| Bangkok | $499–$699/Varies | Up to 3 months; Mon–Sat |
| Beijing | $599–$799/Varies | Up to 3 months; Mon–Sat |
| Dublin | $199–$399/Varies | Up to 30 days; Tue–Sat |
| Frankfurt | $199–$399/Varies | Up to 30 days; Tue–Sat |
| Guatemala City | $150–$350/Varies | 3–30 days; Mon–Fri |
| Hong Kong | $499–$699/Varies | Up to 3 months; Tue–Sat |
| Istanbul | $199–$399/Varies | Up to 30 days; Tue–Sat |
| Jakarta | $599–$799/Varies | Up to 3 months; Mon–Sat |
| Johannesburg | $899/Varies | Up to 45 days; Mon–Sat |
| Madrid | $199–$399/Varies | Up to 30 days; Mon–Sat |
| Manila | $499–$699/Varies | Up to 3 months; Tue–Sat |
| Melbourne | $699–$999/Varies | Up to 3 months; Wed |
| Mexico City | $150–$250/Varies | 3–30 days; Sat–Thu |
| Milan | $199–$399/Varies | 9 days; Mon–Thu |
| Paris | $199–$399/Varies | Up to 30 days; Tue–Sat |
| Rio de Janiero | $399–$499/Varies | Up to 14 days; Mon–Sat |
| Rome | $199–$399/Varies | Up to 30 days; Tue–Sat |
| Saigon | $599–$799/Varies | Up to 3 months; Mon–Sat |
| San Jose | $150–$350/Varies | 3–30 days; Mon–Fri |
| Santiago | $399–$499/Varies | Up to 14 days; Mon–Sat |
| Seoul | $499–$699/Varies | Up to 3 months; Tue–Sat |
| Shanghai | $599–$799/Varies | Up to 3 months; Mon–Sat |
| Singapore | $499–$699/Varies | Up to 3 months; Tue–Sat |
| Sydney | $699–$999/Varies | Up to 3 months; Wed, Sat |
| Taipei | $499–$699/Varies | Up to 3 months/ Tue–Sat |
| Tel Aviv | $599/Varies | Up to 3 months; Mon–Sat |
| Tokyo | $499–$699/Varies | Up to 3 months; Tue–Sat |
| Vienna | $199–$399/Varies | Up to 30 days; Tue–Sat |

**Flights originating from:** New York
**Address:** 169 West 81st Street, New York, NY 10024
**Phone:** (212) 362-3636
**Fax:** (212) 362-3236
**Times to call:** 10AM–5:30PM EST, Mon–Fri
**Recorded information:** Yes
**Type of business:** Courier company
**Annual registration fee:** No
**Courier assignment length:** 3 days to 3 months
**Luggage restrictions:** Carry-on only
**Airlines used:** Sabena, Olympic, Qantas, Garuda, Northwest, Asiana, Aer Lingus, Lufthansa, Turkish, SAA, Iberia, Delta, Alitalia, United, Varig, Vasp, El Al, Austrian

Virtually all international shipping companies use couriers and courier services to send parcels around the world.

**Last-minute discounts:** Yes
**Additional non-courier travel services:** Domestic flights 35% off published fares to connect with your courier flight
**Method of payment:** Money order; personal check; cash
**Credit cards accepted:** Yes, if you are willing to pay a slightly higher fare.
**Comments:** It is difficult to reach DTI by phone. The recorded message suggests that you fax requests to the number above.

# East–West Express

| Destination | Round trip/last-minute fare | Length of stay/Departure days |
|---|---|---|
| **Bangkok** | **$650/No** | **Up to 90 days; Tue–Sat** |
| **Beijing** | **$650/No** | **Up to 90 days; Tue–Sat** |
| **Brisbane** | **$1,600/No** | **Up to 90 days; Tue–Sat** |
| **Cape Town** | **$1,150/No** | **Up to 90 days; Tue–Sat** |
| **Hong Kong** | **$650/No** | **Up to 90 days; Tue–Sat** |
| **Johannesburg** | **$950/No** | **Up to 90 days; Tue–Sat** |
| **Manila** | **$650/No** | **Up to 90 days; Tue–Sat** |
| **Melbourne** | **$1,600/No** | **Up to 90 days; Tue–Sat** |
| **Shanghai** | **$650/No** | **Up to 90 days; Tue–Sat** |
| **Singapore** | **$650/No** | **Up to 90 days; Tue–Sat** |
| **Sydney** | **$1,600/No** | **Up to 90 days; Tue–Sat** |
| **Taipei** | **$650/No** | **Up to 90 days; Tue–Sat** |
| **Tokyo** | **$650/No** | **Up to 90 days; Tue–Sat** |

**Flights originating from:** New York
**Address:** P.O. Box 300849, JFK Airport Station, Jamaica, NY 11430
**Phone:** (718) 656-6246
**Fax:** (718) 656-6247
**Toll-free number:** No
**Point of contact:** Tracy Arato
**Times to call:** 9AM–5PM EST Mon–Fri
**Recorded information:** No
**Type of business:** Courier Company
**Conducting business since:** 1987
**Annual registration fee:** No
**Courier assignment length:** Flexible
**Luggage restrictions:** Carry-on only
**Frequent flyer mileage accrued:** Yes, on Qantas and South African Airways
**Airlines used:** Northwest, Qantas, South African Airways
**Return date flexibility:** Yes—very flexible
**One-way tickets available:** No
**Cancellation phone list:** No
**Last-minute discounts:** No
**Additional non-courier travel services:** No
**Recommended advance reservations:** 2 months
**Earliest possible reservations:** 2 months
**Departure taxes:** Varies at airport
**Deposit:** No
**Method of payment:** Money order; personal check
**Credit cards accepted:** No
**Comments:** This is a helpful company.

## Halbart Express

| Destination | Round trip/last-minute fare | Length of stay/Departure days |
|---|---|---|
| Bangkok | $428–$628/* | 1–3 weeks; Tue–Thu, Sat |
| Brussels | $278–$428/$99 | 1 week; Mon–Thu, Sat |
| Dublin | $220–$378/* | 7 or 8 days; Mon–Thu, Sat |
| Hong Kong | $428–$728/* | 1–3 weeks; Tue–Thu, Sat |
| London | $220–$328/$99 | 7 or 8 days; Mon–Sat |
| Madrid | $220–$378/$99 | 8 or 9 days; Mon–Thu, Sat |
| Manila | $428–$628/$187 | 1–3 weeks;Tue–Thu, Sat |
| Milan | $220–$428/$149 | 1–2 weeks; Mon–Thu, Sat |
| Paris | $250–$450/$99 | 1 week; Mon–Thu, Sat |
| Rome | $220–$428/$99 | 8 or 14 days; Tue–Thu, Sat |
| Singapore | $428–$628/$187 | 1–3 weeks; Tue–Thu, Sat |
| Sydney | $550–$750/* | 2 weeks; Tue, Wed, Sat |
| Taipei | $428–$528/* | 1–3 weeks; Tue–Thu, Sat |
| Tokyo | $428–$528/$187 | 1–4 weeks; Tue–Thu, Sat |

*Information regarding these rates was unavailable at the time of publication.

**Flights originating from:** New York
**Address:** 147-05 176th Street, Jamaica, NY 11434
**Phone:** (718) 656-8189
**Fax:** (718) 917-0717
**Point of contact:** Jeannie, Stephanie, or Amanda
**Times to call:** 9AM–3PM EST Mon–Fri
**Recorded information:** Yes, 24 hours
**Type of business:** Courier company
**Conducting business since:** 1983
**Annual registration fee:** No
**Courier assignment length:** 1 to 3 weeks
**Luggage restrictions:** Carry-on only
**Frequent flyer mileage accrued:** Yes
**Airlines used:** American, TWA, Asiana, Northwest, Aerlingus, Iberia, KLM, Air New Zealand, Alitalia
**Return date flexibility:** No
**One-way tickets available:** Yes, sometimes
**Cancellation phone list:** Yes
**Last-minute discounts:** Yes
**Recommended advance reservations:** 3 to 6 weeks
**Earliest possible reservations:** 2 months
**Departure taxes:** $28
**Deposit:** $100
**Method of payment:** Certified check; money order; cash
**Credit cards accepted:** No
**Comments:** Prices are slightly higher during summer months. Halbart is one of the major players in the courier business.

## Jupiter Air

| Destination | Round trip/last-minute fare | Length of stay/Departure days |
|---|---|---|
| **Hong Kong** | **$400/Varies** | **7–30 days; Tue–Sat** |
| **London** | **$150/Varies** | **7–30 days; Tue–Sat** |
| **Singapore** | **$550/Varies** | **7–30 days; Tue–Sat** |

**Flights originating from:** New York
**Address:** JFK International Airport, Building 14, Jamaica, NY 11430
**Phone:** (718) 656-6050
**Fax:** (718) 656-7263
**Toll-free number:** No
**Point of contact:** Ron or Dania
**Times to call:** 9AM–5:30PM EST Mon–Fri
**Recorded information:** No
**Type of business:** Courier company
**Conducting business since:** 1988
**Annual registration fee:** $35 for 5 years
**Courier assignment length:** 1 to 2 weeks
**Luggage restrictions:** Carry-on only to Singapore; 1 checked bag plus carry-on to Hong Kong
**Frequent flyer mileage accrued:** No
**Airlines used:** JAL, United
**Return date flexibility:** No
**One-way tickets available:** Yes
**Cancellation phone list:** Yes
**Last-minute discounts:** Yes
**Additional non-courier travel services:** No
**Recommended advance reservations:** 1 month
**Earliest possible reservations:** 3 months
**Departure taxes:** No
**Deposit:** $100
**Method of payment:** Certified check; money order; personal check
**Credit cards accepted:** No
**Comments:** Prices are slightly higher during summer months. This is a helpful company. A previous representative stated, "If we do not have a person within two days prior to the flight, we will give the ticket away for FREE." It's hard to do better than that!

# Now Voyager

| Destination | Round trip/last-minute fare | Length of stay/Departure days |
|---|---|---|
| Bangkok | $699/$299 | 7–90 days; Tues–Thu, Sat |
| Buenos Aires | $499/$150 | 7–13 days; Mon, Wed, Thu, Sat |
| Capetown | $1,199/Varies | Up to 90 days |
| Caracas | $230/$99 | 6 –9 days; Sat only |
| Copenhagen | $259/$159 | 1 week; Mon–Thu, Sat |
| Dublin | $299/$200 | 7 or 8 days |
| Frankfurt | Varies/$150 | 7 days |
| Hong Kong | $399–$788/$199 | 7–30 days; Tue–Sat |
| Johannesburg | $999/$499 | Up to 90 days; Wed, Fri, Sat |
| London | $159–259/$150 | 7–30 days; 6 flights per day |
| Madrid | $288/$150 | 7–15 days |
| Manila | $699/$299 | 3–30 days |
| Mexico City | $189/$100 | 3–30 days; Mon–Sun |
| Milan | $339/$149 | 1–2 weeks |
| Paris | $288/$99 | 1 week |
| Puerto Rico | $259/$150 | 6–9 days |
| Rio de Janeiro | $399–$499/$299 | 1–2 weeks |
| Rome | $339/$99 | 1–2 weeks |
| Santiago | $499/Varies | 6–9 days |
| Sao Paulo | $399–$510/$200 | 8–13 days |
| Seoul | $699/Varies | Up to 90 days |
| Singapore | $699/$150 | 7–90 days; Mon–Sat |
| Stockholm | $259/$150 | 3–30 days |
| Taipei | $699/Varies | Up to 90 days |
| Tel Aviv | $775–$875/Varies | Varies |
| Tokyo | $399–$788/$299 | 7–30 days |

**Flights originating from:** New York
**Address:** 74 Varick Street, Suite 307, New York, NY 10013
**Phone:** (212) 431-1616
**Fax:** (212) 334-5243
**Toll-free number:** No
**Point of contact:** Anyone
**Times to call:** 10AM–5:30PM Mon–Fri, 12PM–4:30PM Sat EST
**Recorded information:** 11AM–5:30PM EST Mon–Fri
**Type of business:** Courier Broker
**Conducting business since:** 1983
**Annual registration fee:** $50
**Courier assignment length:** 1 week to 1 month; some flights have open return dates
**Luggage restrictions:** 1 carry-on only
**Frequent flyer mileage accrued:** Yes
**Airlines used:** American, Iberia, JAL, SAS, Northwest, United, Lanchile, Varig, Aero Mexico, South African, KLM
**Return date flexibility:** Yes
**One-way tickets available:** Yes

*The types of items that you will transport include documents, files, boxes, computer disks, contracts, and so on. You will not have to load the material. The courier company takes care of that on both ends.*

**Cancellation phone list:** Yes (Jet-setter program)
**Last-minute discounts:** Yes—one of the best selections in the industry
**Additional non-courier travel services:** Non-courier discount domestic flights
**Recommended advance reservations:** 2 months
**Earliest possible reservations:** 2 months
**Departure taxes:** $28
**Deposit:** $50
**Method of payment:** Certified check; money order; cash
**Credit cards accepted:** Yes
**Comments:** This is an extremely busy company and it is usually difficult to get through on the phone. They offer one of the largest selections of courier flights in the world. Be sure to call the information line prior to talking with an agent. Prices are slightly higher during summer months.

## Virgin Wholesale Express

| Destination | Round trip/last minute fare | Length of stay/Departure days |
|---|---|---|
| **London** | **$330/$300** | **Up to 6 weeks; flights daily** |

**Flights originating from:** New York
**Address:** 149-32 132nd Street, Jamaica, NY 11430
**Phone:** (718) 529-6814
**Fax:** (718) 529-6817
**Toll-free number:** No
**Point of contact:** Janet or Leslie
**Times to call:** 10AM–5PM EST Mon–Fri
**Recorded information:** No
**Type of business:** Courier Broker
**Conducting business since:** 1991
**Annual registration fee:** No
**Courier assignment length:** Up to 6 weeks
**Luggage restrictions:** Carry-on and 2 checked bags
**Frequent flyer mileage accrued:** Yes
**Airlines used:** Virgin Atlantic
**Return date flexibility:** No
**One-way tickets available:** No
**Cancellation phone list:** No
**Last-minute discounts:** No
**Additional non-courier travel services:** No
**Recommended advance reservations:** 2 months
**Earliest possible reservations:** 2 months
**Departure taxes:** Included in price
**Deposit:** No
**Method of payment:** Certified check; money order; personal check
**Credit cards accepted:** Yes

# World Courier

| Destination | Round trip/last-minute fare | Length of stay/Departure days |
|---|---|---|
| **Mexico City** | **$100–$300/No** | **3–30 days; Mon–Thu, Sun** |
| **Milan** | **$100–$300/No** | **9 days; Mon–Thu** |

**Flights originating from:** New York
**Address:** 1313 4th Avenue, New Hyde Park, NY 11040
**Phone:** (516) 354-2600
**Fax:** No
**Toll-free number:** No
**Point of contact:** Barbara
**Times to call:** 9AM–12PM EST Mon–Fri
**Recorded information:** No
**Type of business:** Courier Company
**Conducting business since:** 1976
**Annual registration fee:** No
**Courier assignment length:** 1 to 2 weeks
**Luggage restrictions:** 1 checked bag up to 40 pounds plus carry-on
**Frequent flyer mileage accrued:** No
**Airlines used:** Aeromexico, Lufthansa, Swissair
**Return date flexibility:** No
**One-way tickets available:** No
**Cancellation phone list:** No
**Last-minute discounts:** Yes
**Additional non-courier travel services:** No
**Recommended advance reservations:** 1 month
**Earliest possible reservations:** 2 months
**Departure taxes:** Yes
**Deposit:** Yes
**Method of payment:** Certified check; money order; personal check; cash
**Credit cards accepted:** No
**Comments:** Prices are slightly higher during summer months.

# SAN FRANCISCO

## International Business Couriers

| Destination | Round trip/last-minute fare | Length of stay/Departure days |
|---|---|---|
| **Bangkok** | **$495/Varies** | **10–14 days; Tue–Sat** |
| **Manila** | **$400/Varies** | **2 weeks; Tue–Sat** |

**Flights originating from:** San Francisco
**Address:** 1595 East El Segundo Boulevard, Los Angeles International Airport, Los Angeles, CA 90245
**Phone:** (310) 665-1760
**Fax:** (310) 665-0247
**Toll-free number:** No
**Point of contact:** Yolanda
**Times to call:** 9AM–4PM PST Tue–Fri
**Recorded information:** No
**Type of business:** Courier Broker
**Conducting business since:** 1988
**Annual registration fee:** No
**Courier assignment length:** 10–14 days
**Luggage restrictions:** Carry-on only
**Frequent flyer mileage accrued:** Yes
**Airlines used:** Northwest
**Return date flexibility:** No
**One-way tickets available:** No
**Cancellation phone list:** No
**Last-minute discounts:** Yes
**Additional non-courier travel services:** No
**Recommended advance reservations:** 2 months
**Earliest possible reservations:** 2 months
**Departure taxes:** No
**Deposit:** $500
**Method of payment:** Certified check; money order; cash
**Credit cards accepted:** Yes

# Johnny Air Cargo

| Destination | Round trip/last-minute fare | Length of stay/Departure days |
|---|---|---|
| **Manila** | **$450–$550/No** | **Up to 3 months; Mon, Wed, Fri** |

**Flights originating from:** San Francisco
**Address:** 55 Saint Francis Square, Daly City, CA 94015
**Phone:** (415) 991-7080
**Fax:** (415) 991-7085
**Toll-free number:** No
**Point of contact:** Anyone
**Times to call:** 9AM–5PM PST Mon–Fri
**Recorded information:** No
**Type of business:** Courier Company
**Annual registration fee:** No
**Courier assignment length:** Up to 3 months
**Luggage restrictions:** Carry-on and 1 checked bag
**Frequent flyer mileage accrued:** Varies
**Airlines used:** Philippines Airlines, Northwest, United
**Return date flexibility:** Yes
**One-way tickets available:** No
**Cancellation phone list:** No
**Last-minute discounts:** Varies
**Additional non-courier travel services:** Yes
**Recommended advance reservations:** 2 months
**Earliest possible reservations:** 2 months
**Departure taxes:** No
**Deposit:** Varies
**Method of payment:** Certified check; cash
**Credit cards accepted:** No
**Comments:** Prices are slightly higher during summer months.

## Jupiter Air

| Destination | Round trip/last-minute fare | Length of stay/Departure days |
|---|---|---|
| **Bangkok** | **$370–$470/Varies** | **1–3 weeks; flights daily** |
| **London** | **$335–$385/Varies** | **1–3 weeks; flights daily** |
| **Manila** | **$405–$455/Varies** | **7–30 days; flights daily** |
| **Singapore** | **$400–$535/Varies** | **Up to 30 days; flights daily** |

**Flights originating from:** San Francisco
**Address:** 839 Hinckley Road, Suite A, Burlingame, CA 94010
**Phone:** (415) 697-1773
**Fax:** (415) 697-7892
**Toll-free number:** No
**Point of contact:** Haley Liu
**Times to call:** 9AM–5PM PST Mon–Fri
**Recorded information:** No
**Type of business:** Courier Company
**Conducting business since:** 1988
**Annual registration fee:** $35
**Courier assignment length:** 1 to 2 weeks
**Luggage restrictions:** Carry-on only to Singapore; 1 checked bag to Hong Kong and Seoul
**Frequent flyer mileage accrued:** No
**Airlines used:** JAL, Singapore, Asiana, United
**Return date flexibility:** No
**One-way tickets available:** No
**Cancellation phone list:** Yes
**Last-minute discounts:** Yes
**Additional non-courier travel services:** No
**Recommended advance reservations:** 2 months
**Earliest possible reservations:** 3 months
**Departure taxes:** No
**Deposit:** $100
**Method of payment:** Certified check; money order; personal check; cash
**Credit cards accepted:** No
**Comments:** Prices are slightly higher during summer months.

## UTL Travel

| Destination | Round trip/last-minute fare | Length of stay/Departure days |
|---|---|---|
| **Bangkok** | **$485/$100** | * |
| **Beijing** | **$285/$100** | * |
| **London** | **$335/$100** | * |
| **Manila** | **$450–$535/$100** | **7–30 days; Thu, Fri** |
| **Singapore** | **$435/$100** | **Up to 30 days; Thu only** |

*Not available at the time of publication.

**Flights originating from:** San Francisco
**Address:** 320 Corey Way, South San Francisco, CA 94080
**Phone:** (415) 583-5074
**Fax:** (415) 583-8122
**Toll-free number:** No
**Point of contact:** Any agent
**Times to call:** 9AM–6PM PST Mon–Fri
**Recorded information:** Yes
**Type of business:** Courier Broker
**Conducting business since:** 1988
**Annual registration fee:** No
**Courier assignment length:** 1 to 2 weeks
**Luggage restrictions**: Carry-on only to Singapore; 1 checked bag to Hong Kong and Manila
**Frequent flyer mileage accrued:** No
**Airlines used:** JAL, Singapore, Asiana
**Return date flexibility:** No
**One-way tickets available:** No
**Cancellation phone list:** Yes
**Last-minute discounts:** Yes
**Additional non-courier travel services:** Yes
**Recommended advance reservations:** 2 months
**Earliest possible reservations:** 3 months
**Departure taxes:** No
**Deposit:** $100 or $200
**Method of payment:** Certified check; money order; personal check; cash
**Credit cards accepted:** No
**Comments:** Prices are slightly higher during summer months.

## Virgin Wholesale Express

| Destination | Round trip/last-minute fare | Length of stay/Departure days |
|---|---|---|
| **London** | **$400–530/No** | **Up to 6 weeks; flights daily** |

**Flights originating from:** San Francisco
**Address:** Building 197, JFK International Airport, Jamaica, NY 11430
**Phone:** (718) 244-7244
**Fax:** (718) 244-7240
**Toll-free number:** (888) 839-6683
**Point of contact:** Anyone
**Times to call:** 9AM–5PM EST Mon–Fri
**Recorded information:** No
**Type of business:** Courier Broker
**Conducting business since:** 1991
**Annual registration fee:** No
**Courier assignment length:** Up to 6 weeks
**Luggage restrictions:** Carry-on and 2 checked bags
**Frequent flyer mileage accrued:** Yes
**Airlines used:** Virgin Atlantic
**Return date flexibility:** Yes
**One-way tickets available:** Yes
**Cancellation phone list:** No
**Last-minute discounts:** No
**Additional non-courier travel services:** No
**Recommended advance reservations:** 2 months
**Earliest possible reservations:** 2 months
**Departure taxes:** No
**Deposit:** No
**Method of payment:** Personal check; cash
**Credit cards accepted:** Yes

# WASHINGTON D.C.

## Virgin Wholesale Express

| Destination | Round trip/last-minute fare | Length of stay/Departure days |
|---|---|---|
| **London** | **$330–$340/$300** | **Up to 6 weeks; flights daily** |

**Flights originating from:** Washington D.C.
**Address:** 149-32 132nd Street, Jamaica, NY 11430
**Phone:** (718) 529-6814
**Fax:** (718) 529-6817
**Toll-free number:** No
**Point of contact:** Janet or Leslie
**Times to call:** 10AM–5PM EST Mon–Fri
**Recorded information:** No
**Type of business:** Courier Broker
**Conducting business since:** 1991
**Annual registration fee:** No
**Courier assignment length:** Up to 6 weeks
**Luggage restrictions:** Carry-on and 2 checked bags
**Frequent flyer mileage accrued:** Yes
**Airlines used:** Virgin Atlantic
**Return date flexibility:** No
**One-way tickets available:** No
**Cancellation phone list:** No
**Last-minute discounts:** No
**Additional non-courier travel services:** No
**Recommended advance reservations:** 2 months
**Earliest possible reservations:** 2 months
**Departure taxes:** Included in price
**Deposit:** No
**Method of payment:** Certified check; money order; personal check
**Credit cards accepted:** Yes
**Comments:** For cancellations between one and thirty days you only receive ten percent of your money back; for cancellations more than thirty days in advance you get fifty percent of your money back.

# CANADA

## MONTREAL

### F. B. On Board Courier Services, Inc.

| Destination | Round trip/last-minute fare | Length of stay/Departure days |
|---|---|---|
| **London** | **$525/Varies** | **Up to 30 days; Mon–Thu, Sat** |

**Flights originating from:** Montreal
**Address:** 10105 Ryan Avenue, Dorval, Quebec  H9P 1A2
**Phone:** (514) 631-7925
**Fax:** No
**Toll-free number:** No
**Point of contact:** Roland
**Times to call:** 9AM–12PM EST Mon–Fri
**Recorded information:** No
**Type of business:** Courier Company
**Conducting business since:** 1988
**Annual registration fee:** No
**Courier assignment length:** Up to 1 month
**Luggage restrictions:** Carry-on only
**Frequent flyer mileage accrued:** Yes
**Airlines used:** Air Canada
**Return date flexibility:** Yes
**One-way tickets available:** No
**Cancellation phone list:** No
**Last-minute discounts:** Yes
**Additional non-courier travel services:** No
**Recommended advance reservations:** 1 month
**Earliest possible reservations:** 4 months
**Departure taxes:** No
**Deposit:** No
**Method of payment:** Certified check; money order; cash
**Credit cards accepted:** Only accepted 24–48 hours before flight
**Comments:** Prices are slightly higher during summer months. Prices are in Canadian dollars; mulitply by approximately 0.7 to get US dollars.

# TORONTO

## F. B. On Board Courier Services, Inc.

| Destination | Round trip/last-minute fare | Length of stay/Departure days |
|---|---|---|
| **London** | **$525/Varies** | **Up to 30 days; Mon–Thu, Sat** |

**Flights originating from:** Toronto
**Address:** 10105 Ryan Avenue, Dorval, Quebec H9P 1A2
**Phone:** (514) 631-7925
**Fax:** (514) 633-0735
**Toll-free number:** No
**Point of contact:** Roland
**Times to call:** 9AM–12PM EST Mon–Fri
**Recorded information:** No
**Type of business:** Courier Company
**Conducting business since:** 1988
**Annual registration fee:** No
**Courier assignment length:** 8 to 12 days
**Luggage restrictions:** Carry-on only
**Frequent flyer mileage accrued:** Yes
**Airlines used:** Air Canada
**Return date flexibility:** No
**One-way tickets available:** No
**Cancellation phone list:** No
**Last-minute discounts:** Yes
**Additional non-courier travel services:** Yes
**Recommended advance reservations:** 1 month
**Earliest possible reservations:** 4 months
**Departure taxes:** No
**Deposit:** No
**Method of payment:** Certified check; money order
**Credit cards accepted:** No
**Comments:** Prices are slightly higher during summer months. Prices are in Canadian dollars; multiply by approximately 0.7 to get US dollars. Flights actually originate in Montreal, but this company will allow you to fly free from Toronto to Montreal to catch the flight to London.

# VANCOUVER

## F. B. On Board Courier Services, Inc.

| Destination | Round trip/last-minute fare | Length of stay/Departure days |
|---|---|---|
| **London** | **$590/Varies** | **Up to 30 days; Tue–Sat** |

**Flights originating from:** Vancouver
**Address:** 5200 Miller Road, Suite 117, Richmond, BC  V7B 1X8
**Phone:** (604) 278-1266
**Fax:** (604) 278-5367
**Toll-free number:** No
**Point of contact:** Jim Marshall
**Times to call:** 9AM–11AM or 2PM–4PM PST Mon–Fri
**Recorded information:** No
**Type of business:** Courier Company
**Conducting business since:** 1981
**Annual registration fee:** No
**Courier assignment length:** 7 to 30 days
**Luggage restrictions:** Carry-on only
**Frequent flyer mileage accrued:** Yes
**Airlines used:** Air Canada, Canadian
**Return date flexibility:** No
**One-way tickets available:** No
**Cancellation phone list:** No
**Last-minute discounts:** Yes
**Additional non-courier travel services:** Yes
**Recommended advance reservations:** 3 months
**Earliest possible reservations:** 6 months
**Departure taxes:** $15
**Deposit:** No
**Method of payment:** Certified check; money order; cash
**Credit cards accepted:** No
**Comments:** Prices listed are in Canadian dollars, and are slightly higher during summer months; multiply by approximately 0.7 to get US dollars. Book these flights early. Flights actually originate from Montreal, but this company pays for your flight from Vancouver to make the Montreal connection to London.

# CENTRAL AND SOUTH AMERICA

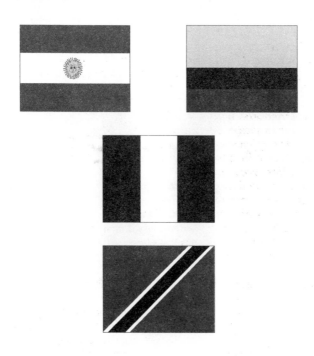

**COURIER COMPANY LISTINGS**

# ARGENTINA

## BUENOS AIRES

### Air Facility

| Destination | Round trip/last-minute fare | Length of stay/Departure days |
|---|---|---|
| Miami | $450/Varies | 3–30 days; Mon–Sat |
| Rio de Janeiro | $150/Varies | 7–8 days |
| Santiago | $50/Varies | 3–30 days; Mon–Fri |
| Sao Paulo | $150/Varies | 3–30 days |

**Flights originating from:** Buenos Aires
**Address:** Almafuerte 42, Barrio 1, Ezeiza, Esteban Echeverria, Prov. de Buenos Aires 1802
**Phone:** 011-54-1-480-9395
**Fax:** 011-54-1-480-9024
**Point of contact:** Paticia
**Type of business:** Courier company
**Courier assignment length:** Up to 30 days
**Airlines used:** Varig
**Recommended advance reservations:** 2 weeks
**Earliest possible reservations:** Twenty days
**Comments:** Flights to Santiago were temporarily suspended at the time of publication.

# ECUADOR

## QUITO

### Tran Air Systems

| Destination | Round trip/last-minute fare | Length of stay/Departure days |
|---|---|---|
| **Miami** | **$250/Varies** | **Up to 21 days; Tue–Sat** |

**Flights originating from:** Quito
**Address:** 7264 NW 25th Street, Miami, FL 33122
**Phone:** (305) 592-1771
**Fax:** (305) 592-2927
**Toll-free number:** No
**Point of contact:** Anyone
**Times to call:** 9:30AM–5:30PM EST Mon–Fri
**Recorded Information:** No
**Type of business:** Courier Company
**Conducting business since:** 1988
**Annual registration fee:** No
**Courier assignment length:** Up to 21 days
**Luggage restrictions:** Carry-on only
**Airlines used:** American
**Return date flexibility:** Yes
**One-way tickets available:** Yes, for US citizens only
**Cancellation phone list:** No
**Last-minute discounts:** Yes
**Additional non-courier travel services:** No
**Recommended advance reservations:** 1 month; 2 months in the summer
**Departure taxes:** No
**Deposit:** $50
**Method of payment:** Money order; cash
**Credit cards accepted:** No
**Comments:** Prices are higher in the summer months. They speak Spanish.

# GUATEMALA

## GUATEMALA CITY

### Tran Air Systems

| Destination | Round trip/last-minute fare | Length of stay/Departure days |
|---|---|---|
| Miami | $280/$180 | Up to 30 days; Tue–Sat |

**Flights originating from:** Guatemala City
**Address:** 7264 NW 25th Street, Miami, FL 33122
**Phone:** (305) 592-1771
**Fax:** (305) 592-2927
**Toll-free number:** No
**Point of contact:** Gloria Arauz
**Times to call:** 9:30AM–5:30PM EST Mon–Fri
**Recorded Information:** No
**Type of business:** Courier Company
**Conducting business since:** 1988
**Annual registration fee:** No
**Courier assignment length:** Up to 30 days
**Luggage restrictions:** Carry-on only
**Frequent flier mileage accrued:** Yes
**Airlines used:** American
**Return date flexibility:** No
**One-way tickets available:** Yes, for US citizens only
**Cancellation phone list:** No
**Last-minute discounts:** Yes
**Additional non-courier travel services:** No
**Recommended advance reservations:** 1 month; 2 months in the summer
**Earliest possible reservations:** 3 months
**Departure taxes:** No
**Deposit:** $50
**Method of payment:** Money order; cash
**Credit cards accepted:** No
**Comments:** Prices are higher in the summer months. They speak Spanish.

# TRINIDAD

## PORT OF SPAIN

### International Business Couriers

| Destination | Round trip/last-minute fare | Length of stay/Departure days |
|---|---|---|
| **Miami** | **$225/No** | **10 days; Mon–Thu, Sat** |

**Flights originating from:** Port of Spain
**Address:** 103 Saint Vincent Street, Port of Spain, Trinidad
**Phone:** (809) 623-4231
**Fax:** (809) 623-4661
**Toll-free number:** No
**Point of contact:** Michelle
**Times to call:** 8:15AM–4PM EST Mon–Fri
**Recorded Information:** No
**Type of business:** Courier Broker
**Annual registration fee:** No
**Courier assignment length:** 10 days
**Luggage restrictions:** Carry-on only
**Frequent flier mileage accrued:** Yes
**Airlines used:** BWA
**Return date flexibility:** No
**One-way tickets available:** No
**Cancellation phone list:** No
**Last-minute discounts:** No
**Additional non-courier travel services:** No
**Recommended advance reservations:** 2 months
**Earliest possible reservations:** 2 months
**Departure taxes:** No
**Deposit:** Half of fare
**Method of payment:** Traveler's check; cash
**Credit cards accepted:** No
**Comments:** This company is friendly, accommodating to travelers' schedules, and easy to work with. However, they usually have very few openings.

# PACIFIC RIM

## COURIER COMPANY LISTINGS

# AUSTRALIA

## SYDNEY

### Jupiter Air

| Destination | Round trip/last-minute fare | Length of stay/Departure days |
|---|---|---|
| **London** | **$1,500–$1,600/Varies** | **Up to 2 months; Mon–Sat** |

**Flights originating from:** Sydney
**Address:** PO Box 224, Mascot, NSW 2020, Australia
**Phone:** 011-61-29-317-2230
**Fax:** 011-61-29-317-3175
**Point of contact:** Robert
**Type of business:** Courier Company
**Conducting business since:** 1988
**Annual registration fee:** No
**Courier assignment length:** Up to 2 months
**Luggage restrictions:** Carry-on only
**Airlines used:** Qantas
**One-way tickets available:** No
**Recommended advance reservations:** 3 months
**Earliest possible reservations:** 3 months
**Departure taxes:** No
**Deposit:** $200
**Method of payment:** Certified check; money order
**Credit cards accepted:** Yes
**Comments:** Fares are listed in Australian dollars; mulitply by approximately 0.64 to get US dollars. One-way flights are available.

# HONG KONG

## Airtropolis Express

| Destination | Round trip/last-minute fare | Length of stay/Departure days |
|---|---|---|
| Jakarta | $2,300/Varies | Up to 30 days |
| Kuala Lumpur | $2,600/Varies | Up to 30 days |
| London | $4,500/Varies | Up to 1 year |
| Singapore | $2,185–$2,585/Varies | Up to 30 days |

**Flights originating from:** Hong Kong
**Address:** Room 315, Air Courier Terminal Office Building, Hong Kong International Airport, Hong Kong, China
**Phone:** 011-852-2751-6186
**Fax:** 011-852-2755-8467
**Point of contact:** Elaine
**Times to call:** 9AM–5PM Hong Kong time (16 hours ahead of PST)
**Recorded information:** No
**Type of business:** Courier Company
**Annual registration fee:** No
**Courier assignment length:** 1 month to 1 year
**Airlines used:** Singapore Air
**Luggage restrictions:** Carry-on only for outbound; 1 checked bag on return flight
**Frequent flier mileage accrued:** No
**Return date flexibility:** Yes
**Cancellation phone list:** Yes
**Last-minute discounts:** Yes
**Additional non-courier travel services:** No
**Recommended advance reservations:** 1 month
**Earliest possible reservations:** 1 month
**Departure taxes:** No
**Deposit:** $1,000
**Method of payment:** Personal check; cash
**Credit cards accepted:** No
**Comments:** Fares are listed in Hong Kong dollars; multiply by approximately 0.12 to get US dollars.

## Bridges Worldwide

| Destination | Round trip/last-minute fare | Length of stay/Departure days |
|---|---|---|
| Bangkok | $1,200–$1,500/$500 | Up to 21 days; Tue–Sun |
| San Francisco | $4,200–$5,800/$1,900 | 2 weeks; Mon–Thu, Sat |
| Sydney | $6,800–$7,200/$3,500 | Up to 2 months |

**Flights originating from:** Hong Kong
**Address:** Room 908, Pacific Trade Center, 2 Kai Hing Road, Kowloon Bay, Hong Kong, China
**Phone:** 011-852-2305-1412
**Fax:** 011-852-2795-8312
**Times to call:** 9:30AM–5PM Hong Kong time (16 hours ahead of PST)
**Point of contact:** Jeanne
**Type of business:** Courier Company
**Annual registration fee:** No
**Courier assignment length:** Up to 1 month
**Airlines used:** Singapore, Qantas, Thai, Air Lanka
**Luggage restrictions:** Carry-on only, except for Sydney
**Return date flexibility:** No
**One-way tickets available:** Yes
**Cancellation phone list:** Yes
**Last-minute discounts:** Yes
**Additional non-courier travel services:** No
**Recommended advance reservations:** 3 months
**Earliest possible reservations:** 6 months
**Departure taxes:** No
**Deposit:** $2,000 refundable deposit for Bangkok flights
**Method of payment:** Certified check; money order; cash
**Credit cards accepted:** No
**Comments:** Fares are listed in Hong Kong dollars; multiply by approximately 0.12 to get US dollars.

## Dyna–Trans Limited

| Destination | Round trip/last-minute fare | Length of stay/Departure days |
|---|---|---|
| **London** | **$6,000/Varies** | **Up to 45 days** |
| **Manila** | **$1,300/Varies** | **Up to 45 days** |

**Flights originating from:** Hong Kong
**Address:** 5th Floor, 152 Queens Road, Central, Hong Kong, China
**Phone:** 011-852-2851-6120
**Fax:** 011-852-2545-3331
**Point of contact:** Gloria Tse
**Type of business:** Courier Company
**Annual registration fee:** No
**Courier assignment length:** Up to 45 days
**Luggage restrictions:** Carry-on and 1 checked bag
**Airlines used:** Virgin Atlantic, Grand International
**Last-minute discounts:** Yes
**Recommended advance reservations:** 2 months
**Earliest possible reservations:** 2 months
**Departure taxes:** No
**Deposit:** No
**Method of payment:** Certified check; money order
**Credit cards accepted:** No
**Comments:** Fares are listed in Hong Kong dollars; multiply by approximately 0.12 to get US dollars.

## Jupiter Air

| Destination | Round trip/last-minute fare | Length of stay/Departure days |
|---|---|---|
| **Chicago** | **$5,000/Varies** | **Mon–Sat** |
| **London** | **$5,000/$3,500** | **Up to 1 month** |
| **Los Angeles** | **$4,000/$1,500** | **Up to 1 month** |
| **New York** | **$5,500/$2,500** | **Up to 1 month** |
| **Osaka** | **$2,200/Varies** | ***** |
| **Singapore** | **$2,100/$1,000** | **Up to 1 month** |

*Information regarding this rate was unavailable at the time of publication.

**Flights originating from:** Hong Kong
**Address:** Room 1701, Tower Number 1, China Hong Kong City, 33 Canton Road, Tsimshatshi, Kowloon, Hong Kong, China
**Phone:** 011-852-2735-1946
**Fax:** 011-852-2735-6450
**Point of contact:** Eve Lai or Jovie Chan
**Type of business:** Courier Company
**Conducting business since:** 1988
**Annual registration fee:** No
**Courier assignment length:** Up to 1 month
**Luggage restrictions:** Some flights allow checked bags
**Airlines used:** Japan, United, Qantas
**Return date flexibility:** No
**One-way tickets available:** No
**Cancellation phone list:** Yes
**Last-minute discounts:** Yes
**Additional non-courier travel services:** No
**Recommended advance reservations:** 2 months
**Earliest possible reservations:** 2 months
**Departure taxes:** No
**Deposit:** $1,000-$2,500 deposit (Hong Kong dollars)
**Method of payment:** Certified check; cash
**Credit cards accepted:** No
**Comments:** Fares are listed in Hong Kong dollars; multiply by approximately 0.12 to get US dollars.

# Linehaul Express

| Destination | Round trip/last-minute fare | Length of stay/Departure days |
|---|---|---|
| **Bangkok** | **$1,000/$500** | **4–14 days; flights daily** |
| **Manila** | **$1,250/$500** | **Up to 30 days; flights daily** |
| **Osaka** | **$2,500/$1,000** | **4–14 days** |
| **Seoul** | **$1,800/$500** | **4–14 days** |
| **Shanghai** | **$1,900/Varies** | **Up to 30 days** |
| **Taipei** | **$1,000/$500** | **4–60 days; flights daily** |
| **Tokyo** | **$2,500/$900** | **4–14 days** |

**Flights originating from:** Hong Kong
**Address:** 33 Canton Road, Hong Kong, China
**Phone:** 011-852-2316-1997
**Fax:** 011-852-2311-2639
**Times to call:** 9:30AM-5:30PM Hong Kong time (16 hours ahead of PST)
**Point of contact:** Matthew Chan, Rosana Leung, Wendy To
**Type of business:** Courier Company
**Conducting business since:** 1989
**Annual registration fee:** No
**Courier assignment length:** Up to 1 month
**Airlines used:** Cathay Pacific
**Luggage restrictions:** Carry-on only
**Return date flexibility:** Yes
**One-way tickets available:** No
**Cancellation phone list:** Yes
**Last-minute discounts:** Yes
**Additional non-courier travel services:** No
**Recommended advance reservations:** 2 months
**Earliest possible reservations:** 6 months
**Departure taxes:** No
**Deposit:** $2,000 deposit (Hong Kong dollars)
**Method of payment:** Cash
**Credit cards accepted:** No
**Comments:** Fares are listed in Hong Kong dollars; multiply by approximately 0.12 to get US dollars.

# JAPAN

## TOKYO

### Fastlink Express

| Destination | Round trip/last-minute fare | Length of stay/Departure days |
|---|---|---|
| **Bangkok** | **¥45,000/No** | **Up to 90 days; Tue** |
| **Hong Kong** | **¥45,000/No** | **Up to 90 days; Tue** |
| **Singapore** | **¥45,000/No** | **Up to 90 days; Tue** |

**Flights originating from:** Tokyo
**Address:** 476 Nanaei, Tomisato-Machi, Ingu-Gun, Chiba-Pre 286-02, Tokyo 108, Japan
**Phone:** 011-81-4-7691-2895
**Fax:** 011-81-4-7691-2895
**Toll-free number:** No
**Point of contact:** Mr. A. Kukinorno or Ms. Yukari Yamaguchi
**Times to call:** 9AM–9PM Tokyo time (17 hours ahead of PST)
**Recorded information:** No
**Type of business:** Courier company
**Annual registration fee:** No
**Courier assignment length:** Up to 90 days
**Luggage restrictions:** Carry-on only
**Airlines used:** Northwest
**Return date flexibility:** Yes
**One-way tickets available:** No
**Cancellation phone list:** No
**Last-minute discounts:** No
**Additional Non-courier travel services:** No
**Recommended advance reservations:** 1 to 2 months
**Earliest possible reservations:** 2 months
**Departure taxes:** No
**Deposit:** No
**Method of payment:** Cash only
**Credit cards accepted:** No
**Comments:** Fares are listed in Yen; mulitply by approximately 0.0076 to get US dollars.

## Wholesale Courier

| Destination | Round trip/last-minute fare | Length of stay/Departure days |
|---|---|---|
| **Bangkok** | **¥45,000/Varies** | **Up to 3 months; Mon–Fri, Sun** |
| **Hong Kong** | **¥45,000/Varies** | **Up to 3 months; flights daily** |
| **Singapore** | **¥45,000/Varies** | **Up to 3 months; Mon–Sat** |

**Flights originating from:** Tokyo
**Address:** 2-20-14 Tsurumatsu Building 2F, Hiroshidai, Tomisato-machi, Inba-gun Chiba 286-02, Tokyo, Japan
**Phone:** 011-81-4-7692-0311
**Fax:** 011-81-4-7692-0309
**Toll-free number:** No
**Point of contact:** Mr. Endo
**Recorded information:** No
**Type of business:** Courier Company
**Annual registration fee:** No
**Courier assignment length:** 3 months
**Luggage restrictions:** Carry-on only
**Frequent flier mileage accrued:** No
**Airlines used:** Northwest
**Return date flexibility:** Yes
**One-way tickets available:** No
**Cancellation phone list:** Yes
**Last-minute discounts:** Yes; as low as ¥10,000
**Additional non-courier travel services:** No
**Earliest possible reservations:** 3 months
**Departure taxes:** ¥20,000
**Deposit:** No
**Method of payment:** Cash only
**Credit cards accepted:** No
**Comments:** This company has flights available every day. Fares are listed in Yen; mulitply by approximately 0.0076 to get US dollars.

# NEW ZEALAND

## AUKLAND

### TNT Express Worldwide

| Destination | Round trip/last-minute fare | Length of stay/Departure days |
|---|---|---|
| Frankfurt | $2,300/No | Up to 6 months; flights daily |
| Honolulu | $1,550/No | Up to 6 months |
| London | $2,300/No | Up to 6 months |
| Los Angeles | $1,450/No | Up to 2 months; 6 days a week |
| San Francisco | $1,550/No | Up to 2 months |
| Seattle | $1,550/No | Up to 2 months |
| Vancouver | $1,600/No | Up to 6 months |

**Flights originating from:** Aukland
**Address:** PO Box 73122, Aukland International Airport, Aukland, New Zealand
**Phone:** 011-64-9-275-0549
**Fax:** 011-64-9-275-4567
**Toll-free number:** No
**Point of contact:** Christine Toopi
**Recorded information:** No
**Type of business:** Courier Company
**Annual registration fee:** No
**Courier assignment length:** Up to 6 months
**Luggage restrictions:** Varies
**Airlines used:** Air New Zealand
**Return date flexibility:** Yes
**One-way tickets available:** Yes
**Additional non-courier travel services:** No
**Recommended advance reservations:** 2 months
**Earliest possible reservations:** 2 months
**Departure taxes:** No
**Deposit:** $300 (New Zealand dollars)
**Method of payment:** Certified check; money order
**Comments:** Fares are listed in New Zealand dollars; mulitply by approximately 0.56 to get US dollars.

# SINGAPORE

## Air United

| Destination | Round trip/last-minute fare | Length of stay/Departure days |
|---|---|---|
| **Bangkok** | **$200/No** | **Up to 30 days** |
| **Hong Kong** | **$450/No** | **Up to 14 days** |
| **Los Angeles** | **$800/No** | **Up to 30 days** |
| **Manila** | **$500/No** | **Up to 30 days** |
| **San Francisco** | **$800/No** | **Up to 30 days** |

**Flights originating from:** Singapore
**Address:** 150 Orchard Road #03-70, Orchard Plaza, Singapore 238841
**Phone:** 011-65-735-7684
**Fax:** 011-65-735-7584
**Toll-free number:** No
**Point of contact:** Karen Ho or Fizah
**Times to call:** 10AM–6PM Singapore time (15 hours ahead of PST)
**Recorded information:** No
**Type of business:** Courier Company
**Annual registration fee:** No
**Courier assignment length:** Up to 30 days
**Luggage restrictions:** Carry-on and 1 checked bag
**Frequent flyer mileage accrued:** No, except on Qantas
**Airlines used:** United, JAL, Qantas, and Singapore Air
**Return date flexibility:** No
**One-way tickets available:** Yes, for some flights
**Cancellation phone list:** No
**Last-minute discounts:** Yes
**Additional non-courier travel services:** No
**Recommended advance reservations:** 1 month
**Earliest possible reservations:** 2 to 3 months
**Departure taxes:** No
**Deposit:** $150–$250
**Method of payment:** Personal check; cash
**Credit cards accepted:** No
**Comments:** Fares are listed in Singapore dollars; multiply by approximately 0.62 to get US dollars. There are also one-way daily flights to Kuala Lumpur for S$65.

# Airpak Express Pte. Ltd.

| Destination | Round trip/last-minute fare | Length of stay/Departure days |
|---|---|---|
| **Manila** | **$300/No** | **1 day; flights daily** |

**Flights originating from:** Singapore
**Address:** 48 MacTaggart Road, Unit 05-04, Singapore 368088
**Phone**: 011-65-383-9200 or 011-65-282-3119
**Fax:** 011-65-282-0091
**Point of contact:** Sam Anson
**Type of business:** Courier company
**Courier assignment length:** One day
**Luggage restrictions:** Carry-on, but you can pay a fee for checked bags
**Airlines used:** Philippine Airlines
**Return date flexibility:** No
**One-way tickets available:** No
**Cancellation phone list:** No
**Last-minute discounts:** No
**Additional non-courier travel services:** Yes
**Recommended advance reservations:** Call about one week before preferred departure date for flight availability
**Earliest possible reservations:** Call any time
**Departure taxes:** Yes
**Deposit:** No
**Method of payment:** Certified check; money order; cash
**Credit cards accepted:** No
**Comments:** Although this company most often books flights to Manila, they also handle flights to 30 other cities. Call for flight availability. If you already hold a ticket to Manila from Singapore, ask about their need for couriers that day. They will pay the difference between $300 and the face value of your ticket. Your ticket does not have to be on Philippine Airlines. Fares are listed in Singapore dollars; mulitiply by approximately 0.62 to get US dollars.

# Airtropolis

| Destination | Round trip/last-minute fare | Length of stay/Departure days |
|---|---|---|
| **Bangkok** | **$200–$250/No** | **3–14 days; flights daily** |

**Flights originating from:** Singapore
**Address:** SATS Express and Courier Centre, Unit #01-04, Singapore Changi Airport, Singapore 819459
**Phone:** 011-65-545-3686
**Fax:** 011-65-545-2055
**Toll-free number:** No
**Point of contact:** Phya Travel Service
**Times to call:** 9AM to 5PM Singapore time (15 hours ahead of PST)
**Recorded information:** No
**Type of business:** Courier Company
**Courier assignment length:** Up to 2 weeks
**Luggage restrictions:** 1 carry-on bag only
**Airlines used:** Sinapore Air, Alitalia
**Return date flexibility:** Yes
**Additional non-courier travel services:** No
**Recommended advance reservations:** 2 months
**Earliest possible reservations:** 2 months
**Deposit:** Varies
**Method of payment:** Certified check; money order
**Comments:** This company prefers that you book flights through Phya Travel Services. One-way flights also available to Kuala Lumpur for around $80. Fares are listed in Singapore dollars; multiply by approximately 0.62 to get US dollars.

## Concord Express

| Destination | Round trip/last-minute fare | Length of stay/Departure days |
|---|---|---|
| **Bangkok** | **$150/No** | **Up to 2 weeks; flights daily** |

**Flights originating from:** Singapore
**Address:** Cargo Agent, Building C, Unit 01-06/08, Airport Cargo Road, Singapore
**Phone:** 011-65-542-2894
**Fax:** 011-65-542-2649
**Point of contact:** Phya Travel Service (see Phya listing)
**Times to call:** 9AM to 5PM Singapore time (15 hours ahead of PST)
**Type of business:** Courier company
**Annual registration fee:** No
**Courier assignment length:** Up to 2 weeks
**Frequent flyer mileage accrued:** Yes
**Airlines used:** Singapore Airlines
**Return date flexibility:** Yes
**One-way tickets available:** Yes
**Cancellation phone list:** No
**Last-minute discounts:** No
**Additional non-courier travel services:** No
**Recommended advance reservations:** 3 weeks
**Earlist possible reservations:** Reservations are on a first come, first serviced basis
**Deposit:** No
**Method of payment:** Cash only
**Credit cards accepted:** No
**Comments:** Concord is affiliated with OBC in Bangkok. They book only through Phya. They don't want couriers contacting them directly. Concord also offers one-way flights to Kale for $50. Fares are listed in Singapore dollars; multiply by approximately 0.62 to get US dollars.

## Phya Travel Service

| Destination | Round trip/last-minute fare | Length of stay/Departure days |
|---|---|---|
| **Bangkok** | **$180–$250/No** | **3-14 days; flights daily** |

**Flights originating from :** Singapore
**Address:** 01-18 Golden Mile Complex, Beach Road, Singapore 199588
**Phone:** 011-65-294-5415 or 011-65-295-4850
**Fax:** 011-65-296-1808
**Point of contact:** Steven Ong
**Times to call:** 9AM to 5PM Singapore time (15 hours ahead of PST)
**Type of business:** Travel agent
**Annual registration fee:** No
**Courier assignment length:** Varies
**Frequent flyer mileage accrued:** Yes
**One-way tickets available:** Yes
**Cancellation phone list:** No
**Last-minute discounts:** Yes
**Additional non-courier travel services:** No
**Recommended advance reservations**: 1 month
**Departure taxes:** Yes
**Deposit:** No
**Method of payment:** Cash only
**Credit cards accepted:** No
**Comments:** Phya is the recommended primary contact for courier bookings with Airtropolis and Concord in Singapore; see their respective listings for more information. Ask Phya about hotel services if you need help with lodging in Bangkok or other places in Thailand. Prices are listed in Singapore dollars; multiply by approximately 0.62 to get US dollars.

# SOUTH KOREA

## SEOUL

### Jupiter Express

| Destination | Round trip/last-minute fare | Length of stay/Departure days |
|---|---|---|
| **Los Angeles** | **$350–$400/No** | **Up to 30 days; flights daily** |

**Flights originating from:** Seoul
**Address:** PO Box 8705, Seoul, Korea 682-3
**Phone:** 011-82-2-665-6024
**Fax:** 011-82-2-665-1777
**Point of contact:** Mr. Jung
**Times to call:** 9AM–5PM Korea time (17 hours ahead of PST)
**Recorded information:** No
**Type of business:** Courier Broker
**Annual registration fee:** No
**Courier assignment length:** Up to 30 days
**Luggage restrictions:** Carry-on and 1 checked bag
**Airlines used:** Asiana
**Return date flexibility:** Yes
**Last-minute discounts:** Yes
**Recommended advance reservations:** 2 months
**Earliest possible reservations:** 2 months
**Departure taxes:** No
**Deposit:** Yes
**Method of payment:** Certified check; money order

# THAILAND

## BANGKOK

### Bridges Worldwide

| Destination | Round trip/last-minute fare | Length of stay/Departure days |
|---|---|---|
| **Singapore** | **ß3,000/No** | **2 weeks to 1 year** |

**Flights originating from:** Bangkok
**Address:** 180-71 Vibharvdi Rangsit Road, Donmuang, Bangkok
**Phone:** 011-66-2-533-4066 or 011-66-2-533-9744
**Fax:** 011-66-2-533-6179
**Point of contact:** Siriporn
**Type of business:** Courier company
**Courier assignment length:** Varies
**Luggage restrictions:** Carry-on only
**Airlines used:** Air New Zealand
**Recommended advance reservations:** 2 weeks
**Credit cards accepted:** No
**Comments:** Fares are listed in Bhat; multiply by approximately 0.023 to get US dollars.

## OBC Courier

| Destination | Round trip/last-minute fare | Length of stay/Departure days |
|---|---|---|
| **Singapore** | **฿4,000/No** | **Up to 14 days; Fri** |

**Flights originating from:** Bangkok
**Address:** Vanit Building #1, 16th Floor, Room 1605, 1126/1 New Petchburi, Bangkok 10400 Thailand
**Phone:** 011-66-2-255-8590
**Fax:** 011-66-2-255-8593
**Toll-free number:** No
**Point of contact:** Charlie or Jintana
**Times to call:** 9AM–6PM Bangkok time (15 hours ahead of PST)
**Recorded information:** No
**Type of business:** Courier Company
**Annual registration fee:** No
**Courier assignment length:** 14 days
**Luggage restrictions:** Carry-on only
**Frequent flyer mileage accrued:** Yes
**Airlines used:** Singapore Air
**Return date flexibility:** Yes
**One-way tickets available:** Yes
**Cancellation phone list:** No
**Last-minute discounts:** No
**Additional non-courier travel services:** No
**Earliest possible reservations:** 1 month
**Departure taxes:** ฿20
**Deposit:** No
**Method of payment:** Cash only
**Credit cards accepted:** Yes
**Comments:** Must book and pay 10 days in advance. Fares are listed in Bhat; multiply by approximately 0.023 to get US dollars.

# Siam Trans International

| Destination | Round trip/last-minute fare | Length of stay/Departure days |
|---|---|---|
| **Hong Kong** | **฿4,500/No** | **Up to 14 days** |
| **Los Angeles** | **฿15,000/No** | **Up to 30 days** |
| **San Francisco** | **฿15,000/No** | **Up to 30 days** |

**Flights originating from:** Bangkok
**Address:** 78 Kiatnakin Building, Bushland, New Road, Bangkok 10500 Thailand
**Phone:** 011-66-2-235-6741
**Fax:** 011-66-2-236-1042
**Toll-free number:** No
**Point of contact:** Sirirat
**Times to call:** 10AM–6PM Bangkok time (15 hours ahead of PST)
**Recorded information:** No
**Type of business:** Courier Company
**Annual registration fee:** No
**Courier assignment length:** Up to 14 days
**Luggage restrictions:** Carry-on only
**Frequent flyer mileage accrued:** No
**Airlines used:** Thai, Qantas, Canadian, JAL
**Return date flexibility:** Yes
**One-way tickets available:** Yes
**Cancellation phone list:** No
**Last-minute discounts:** No
**Additional non-courier travel services:** No
**Recommended advance reservations:** 2 weeks
**Earliest possible reservations:** 1 month
**Departure taxes:** No
**Deposit:** No
**Method of payment:** Cash only
**Credit cards accepted:** No
**Comments:** It's best to check availability on the first of each month. Fares are listed in Baht; multiply by approximately 0.023 to get US dollars.

# EUROPE

**COURIER COMPANY LISTINGS**

# UNITED KINGDOM

## LONDON

### Bridges Worldwide

| Destination | Round trip/last-minute fare | Length of stay/Departure days |
|---|---|---|
| Bangkok | £329/£99 | Up to 1 year; Tue–Sat |
| Beijing | £320/Varies | 7–30 days |
| Los Angeles | £199–£399/Varies | 7 days to 3 months; Thu–Sat |
| New York | £165–£275/Varies | 7 days to 3 months; Tue–Sat |
| Osaka | £450–£580/Varies | 7 days to 3 months; Tue, Thu, Sat |
| Seoul | £299/Varies | Up to 30 days; Tue–Sat |
| Tokyo | £420–£499/Varies | Up to 30 days; Tue–Sun |

**Flights originating from:** London
**Address:** Old Mill House, Mill Road, West Drayton, Middlesex UB7 7EJ
**Phone:** 011-44-1-895-465-065
**Fax:** 011-44-1-895-465-100
**Point of contact:** Keith Madden
**Times to call:** 9AM–5PM U.K. time (8 hours ahead of PST)
**Recorded information:** No
**Type of business:** Courier Broker
**Conducting business since:** 1991
**Courier assignment length:** Up to 1 month
**Luggage restrictions:** Carry-on and 1 checked bag
**Frequent flyer mileage accrued:** No
**Airlines used:** Virgin Gulf, Thai, China, American, Finnair, Lufthansa
**Return date flexibility:** No
**One-way tickets available:** Sometimes
**Last-minute discounts:** Yes
**Additional non-courier travel services:** Non-courier discount flights
**Recommended advance reservations:** 3 weeks
**Earliest possible reservations:** 2 to 3 months
**Departure taxes:** No
**Deposit:** No
**Method of payment:** Certified check; cash
**Credit cards accepted:** Yes
**Comments:** The company must receive full payment before your booking is confirmed. All prices are in pounds sterling; multiply by approximately 1.6 to get US dollars.

# British Airways Travel Shops

| Destination | Round trip/last-minute fare | Length of stay/Departure days |
|---|---|---|
| **Amman** | *£80–£120/Varies* | *1 to 2 weeks* |
| **Bahrain** | *£120–£180/Varies* | *1 to 2 weeks* |
| **Bangkok** | *£349–£360/Varies* | *1 to 2 weeks* |
| **Boston** | *£100–£140/Varies* | *1 to 2 weeks* |
| **Budapest** | *£80–£100/Varies* | *1 to 2 weeks* |
| **Buenos Aires** | *£320–£480/Varies* | *1 to 2 weeks* |
| **Cairo** | *£120–£180/Varies* | *1 to 2 weeks* |
| **Chicago** | *£100–£140/Varies* | *1 to 2 weeks* |
| **Dubai** | *£120–£180/Varies* | *1 week* |
| **Gaborone** | *£300–£450/Varies* | *1 to 2 weeks* |
| **Geneva** | *£60–£90/Varies* | *1 to 2 weeks* |
| **Harare** | *£200–£300/Varies* | *1 to 2 weeks* |
| **Hong Kong** | *£435–£650/Varies* | *1 to 2 weeks* |
| **Johannesburg** | *£400–£600/Varies* | *1 to 2 weeks* |
| **Kuala Lumpur** | *£385–£525/Varies* | *1 to 2 weeks* |
| **Larnaca** | *£69–£105/Varies* | *1 to 2 weeks* |
| **Lisbon** | *£60–£90/Varies* | *1 to 2 weeks* |
| **Mauritius** | *£375–£510/Varies* | *15 days* |
| **Mexico City** | *£300–£450/Varies* | *1 to 2 weeks* |
| **Miami** | *£200–£300/Varies* | *1 to 2 weeks* |
| **Montreal** | *£100–£150/Varies* | *1 week* |
| **Nairobi** | *£300–£450/Varies* | *1 to 2 weeks* |
| **New York** | *£100–£140/Varies* | *1 to 2 weeks* |
| **Newark** | *£100–£140/Vaires* | *1 to 2 weeks* |
| **Philadelphia** | *£100–£140/Varies* | *1 to 2 weeks* |
| **San Francisco** | *£150–£225/Varies* | *2 weeks* |
| **Seattle** | *£150–£225/Varies* | *1 to 2 weeks; Fri, Sat* |
| **Singapore** | *£320–£480/Varies* | *1 to 2 weeks* |
| **Tel Aviv** | *£99–£149/Varies* | *1 to 2 weeks* |
| **Tokyo** | *£250–£360/Varies* | *1 to 2 weeks* |
| **Toronto** | *£120–£180/Varies* | *1 to 2 weeks* |
| **Warsaw** | *£80–£120/Varies* | *1 to 2 weeks* |
| **Washington** | *£100–£150/Varies* | *1 to 2 weeks* |
| **Zurich** | *£60–£90/Varies* | *1 to 2 weeks* |

**Flights originating from:** London
**Address:** World Cargo Centre, 1st Floor, Export Cargo Terminal S126, Heathrow Airport, Hounslow, Middlesex TW6 2JS, U.K.
**Phone:** 011-44-1-815-647-009
**Fax:** 011-44-1-815-626-177
**Toll-free number:** No
**Point of contact:** Reservations
**Times to call:** 9AM–5PM U.K. time (8 hours ahead of PST)
**Recorded information:** No
**Type of business:** Airline/Courier/Freight
**Conducting business since:** 1985
**Annual registration fee:** No

**Courier assignment length:** 1 to 3 weeks
**Luggage restrictions:** 1 carry-on and 1 checked bag
**Frequent flyer mileage accrued:** Yes
**Airlines used:** British Airways
**Return date flexibility:** No
**One-way tickets available:** Yes
**Cancellation phone list:** No
**Last-minute discounts:** Yes
**Additional non-courier travel services:** Yes
**Recommended advance reservations:** 2 to 3 months
**Earliest possible reservations:** 2 to 3 months
**Departure taxes:** Included in price
**Deposit:** No
**Method of payment:** Certified check; money order; cash
**Credit cards accepted:** Yes
**Comments:** A dress code is strictly enforced—no jeans allowed. No refunds or cancellations are accepted. All prices are in pounds sterling; multiply by approximately 1.6 to get US dollars.

# Jupiter Air UK

| Destination | Round trip/last-minute fare | Length of stay/Departure days |
|---|---|---|
| **New York** | **£150/Varies** | **1 to 3 months; Mon–Sat** |
| **Sydney** | **£550 /Varies** | **1 to 3 months; Mon–Sat** |

**Flights originating from:** London
**Address:** Jupiter House, Horton Road, Coinbrook, Slough SL3 OBBB, U.K.
**Phone:** 011-44-1-753-689-989
**Fax:** 011-44-1-753-681-661
**Toll-free number:** No
**Point of contact:** Hellen
**Times to call:** 9AM–5PM U.K. time (8 hours ahead of PST)
**Recorded information:** No
**Type of business:** Courier company
**Annual registration fee:** No
**Courier assignment length:** 1 to 3 months
**Luggage restrictions:** Carry-on and 1 checked bag
**Frequent flyer mileage accrued:** Yes
**Airlines used:** United
**Return date flexibility:** Yes
**One-way tickets available:** Sometimes
**Cancellation phone list:** No
**Last-minute discounts:** Sometimes
**Additional non-courier travel services:** No
**Earliest possible reservations:** 2 months
**Departure taxes:** Included in fare
**Deposit:** £150
**Method of payment:** Personal check; cash
**Credit cards accepted:** Mastercard and Visa
**Comments:** The staff is very helpful and friendly. The London to New York route is a popular flight so try to book 1 month in advance. Fares are listed in pounds sterling; multiply by approximately 1.6 to get US dollars.

## Nomad Courier Service

| Destination | Round trip/last-minute fare | Length of stay/Departure days |
|---|---|---|
| **New York** | **£125–£280/Varies** | **Up to 1 month; Mon–Sat** |

**Flights originating from:** London
**Address:** 664 Hanworth Road, Hounslow, Middlesex TW4 5NP, U.K.
**Phone:** 011-44-1-818-933-820
**Fax:** 011-44-1-818-982-117
**Toll-free number:** No
**Point of contact:** Chris or Dave
**Times to call:** 9AM–5PM U.K. time (8 hours ahead of PST)
**Recorded information:** No
**Type of business:** Courier Service
**Annual registration fee:** No
**Courier assignment length:** Up to 1 month
**Luggage restrictions:** Carry-on; can check up to 2 bags for £10 each
**Airlines used:** American
**Return date flexibility:** Yes
**One-way tickets available:** No
**Last-minute discounts:** Yes
**Additional non-courier travel services:** Yes
**Recommended advance reservations:** 1 month
**Earliest possible reservations:** 6 months
**Deposit:** No
**Method of payment:** Personal check; cash
**Credit cards accepted:** Yes
**Comments:** Fares are listed in pounds sterling; multiply by approximately 1.6 to get US dollars.

# Virgin Wholesale Express

| Destination | Round trip/last-minute fare | Length of stay/Departure days |
|---|---|---|
| Johannesburg | £450–£499/Varies | Up to 3 months; Wed–Mon |
| Los Angeles | £275–£380/Varies | Up to 6 weeks; flights daily |
| Melbourne | £550–£699/Varies | Up to 3 months; Tue, Fri |
| New York | £180–£275/Varies | Up to 6 weeks; flights twice daily |
| Newark | £180–£275/Varies | Up to 6 weeks; flights daily |
| San Francisco | £275–£380/Varies | Up to 6 weeks; flights daily |
| Sydney | £550–£699/Varies | Up to 3 months; Wed–Thu, Sat–Mon |
| Tokyo | £499–£599/£400 | Up to 3 months; Thu–Tue |
| Washington | £235–£275/Varies | Up to 6 weeks; flights daily |

**Flights originating from:** London
**Address:** Unit 8, Radius Park, Faggs Road, Feltham Middlesex TW 14 ONG, U.K.
**Phone:** 011-1-818-975-130
**Fax:** 011-1-818-975-133
**Point of contact:** Stuart Martin
**Type of business:** Courier company
**Courier assignment length:** Up to 3 months
**Luggage restrictions:** 1 checked bag up to 23 kilograms (51 pounds)
**Frequent flyer mileage accrued:** No
**One-way tickets available:** Melbourne, Sydney, and Tokyo
**Last-minute discounts:** Yes
**Method of payment:** Personal check
**Credit cards accepted:** Yes
**Comments:** October and November are the best months for bargain fares. Fares are listed in pounds sterling; multiply by approximately 1.6 to get US dollars.

# PART III

# RESOURCES

# FOR THE COURIER

The following pages provide you with a wealth of travel information. As an air courier, once you reach your destination, you'll have the same needs as other travelers. We've listed contact information for all kinds of travel-related organizations—from auto drive away companies to international hostels and hotels. We've included information on obtaining a visa and passport, as well as lists of travel companies, international tourist offices, recommended travel books, travel bookstores, and more. You can use these organizations to help you plan an exciting adventure abroad.

## TRAVEL COMPANIES

The following is a list of travel companies that could save you money on international and domestic travel.

**Access International, Ltd.** .................................................. (800) 917-7880

**Air Brokers International, Inc.** ........................................... (800) 883-3273
   *Specializes in around-the-world trips*

**Apex Travel, Inc.** ................................................................. (800) 666-0025
   *Specializes in discount airfares to Asia*

**Express Holidays** ................................................................ (800) 266-8669
   *Discounts up to 50 percent*

**Euro-Asia Express** .............................................................. (800) 782-9625
   *Specializes in discount airfares to Asia and some to Europe*

**Discount Travel International** ........................................... (800) 900-7681
   *Up to 60 percent discounts on all types of travel*
   *$45 annual membership fee*

**Preferred Traveler's Club** .................................................. (800) 638-8976

**Europe Through the Back Door, Inc.** ............................... (425) 771-8303
   *Carries many travel books*
   *Offers Eurail/Britrail passes, youth hostel guides, and many other services needed for European travel*

**Fellowship Travel International** ....................................... (800) 446-7667
*Low cost international fares*
*Call between 9am and 5pm EST*

**Student Flights** ........................................................................ (602) 951-1700
*Specializes in low cost flights to most cities in Europe*
*Offers Eurail/Britrail passes, youth hostel guides, and many other services*
*needed for European travel*
*Organization that has helped students for over 35 years*
*Call for their current catalog and prices*

**Japan Budget Travel** ............................................................. (800) 722-0797

**Last Minute Travel Club** ...................................................... (800) 527-8646
*Great fares from the East Coast to Europe*
*Outstanding deals from the East Coast to Mexico or the Caribbean*

**CWT Vacations** ....................................................................... (800) 223-6862
*Great fares to Europe and India*

**Moment's Notice, Inc.** ........................................................... (212) 486-0500

**Pan Express Travel, Inc.** ....................................................... (212) 719-9292

**Travel Avenue** ........................................................................ (800) 333-3335
*Heavily discounted airfares to Europe.*
*Around-the-world airfares for as little as $1569*

**Traveler's Advantage** ........................................................... (800) 548-1116
*Sells unsold space on charter flights, cruises, and tours*

**Uni Travel** ............................................................................... (800) 325-2222
*Discounted international and domestic airfares*

**Virgin Atlantic Airways** ...................................................... (800) 862-8621
*Usually the most inexpensive airlines to Europe*

**Worldwide Discount Travel Club** ....................................... (305) 534-2082

## *Using Travel Companies*

Travel companies typically offer international flights for twenty to thirty percent less than normal economy fares. Although this is an economical way to travel, be aware that ticket deliveries are notoriously slow, and refunds can be made only through the travel company.

## DEPARTURE CITIES

All courier flights leave from the cities listed. It is your responsibility to get to the departure city. If you happen to live in or near New York, Los Angeles, Toronto, Miami, or San Francisco, there are ample flights departing from those cities. For the rest of us who do not live in those cities, we need to find our way to one of the many departure cities. If you live anywhere near New York (by anywhere I mean east of the Mississippi) it is to your advantage to get to New York. Your best savings are from New York. If you live in the western part of the United States, then Los Angeles or San Francisco should be your goal.

**Southwest Airlines** is a good option. Their fares are usually the cheapest in the United States. Call them at (800) 435-9792.

**America West** is another good choice for inexpensive flights. Call them at (800) 235-9292. They offer flights to New York and Los Angeles from most of the United States.

## AUTO DRIVE AWAY COMPANIES

Another option is an auto drive away company. This is where you agree to transport a car for a company from one location to another. The main advantage to doing this is free transportation. You are only responsible for the gas and your expenses. It does not cost you anything to do this. The company will provide you with a free car. There are opportunities to drive expensive cars across all or part of America. If you have ever wanted to drive across the country in a Lexus, BMW, or Mercedes, this could be your chance.

Auto drive away companies give you plenty of time to get across the country. An example is eight to nine days to drive from New York to Los Angeles. This would give you an opportunity for some great sightseeing. Drivers are always in demand by drive away companies, and they can even arrange a return car after your courier flight (remember that this is why you bought this book in the first place).

This is a great opportunity to bring a couple of friends to a departure city for courier flights. Two or three people could pick up a car in one city and drop it off in New York or Los Angeles and catch a courier flight. It is possible to travel around the world for free or next to nothing. You can't do much better than that!

**Auto DriveAway Company** ............................................... **(800) 346-2277**

- *85 offices nationwide; New York (212) 967-2344, Los Angeles (213) 661-6100, Chicago (312) 939-3600, Miami (954) 456-2285*
- *Drivers must be 21 years of age and have a valid driver's license.*
- *Depending on the office, deposits range from $250 to $350 and up. It is refundable by any office and can be paid by cash or traveler's checks.*
- *Foreign drivers are welcome.*
- *Drivers are always in demand.*

**A. Anthony's Driveaway and Truckaway Co., Inc.**

- *Offices nationwide; Florida (954) 970-7384; New Jersey (301) 777-8100, Los Angeles (714) 372-2266, Dallas (214) 823-2820, Denver (303) 893-6101, Washington, DC (540) 349-8471*
- *Drivers must be 21 years of age and have a valid driver's license.*
- *A $200 deposit is required.*
- *Passengers are allowed but must complete registration forms.*

**National Auto Transporters, Inc.**

- *Offices nationwide; Chicago (773) 489-3500, Miami (305) 945-0101, Los Angeles (310) 670-SHIP, Phoenix (602) 992-5200*
- *Drivers must be 21 years of age and have a valid driver's license.*
- *A $285 deposit is required.*
- *Cash or certified check.*
- *There is a $30 nonrefundable registration fee.*
- *Passengers are allowed with references.*

---

## *Auto Drive Away Companies: What you should know*

- *You will need a valid driver's license.*
- *Most of the time you will be asked for a deposit using a credit card or cash.*
- *Some companies have age requirements.*
- *Often there will be mileage and time restrictions.*

## FREIGHTER TRAVEL

Freighter travel is slow and fairly inexpensive. This type of travel is gaining in popularity once again; however, you must be flexible with your travel plans. It was this type of travel that gave us the expression "slow boat to China." The following are a couple of freighter companies:

**Columbus Lines** ..................................................... **(212) 432-1700**
*Ships leave from both U.S. coasts destined for Australia and New Zealand.*

**Lykes Lines**........................................................... **(800) 535-1861**
*Ships leave from the East Coast of the U.S. destined for Africa and the Mediterranean.*

The following is a list of a number of the books or newsletters available on freighter travel:

**Ford's Freighter Travel Guide** .......................................... **(818) 701-7414**
19448 Londelius Street, Northridge, CA 91324
*$24 for an annual subscription.*

**Freighter World Cruises** .................................................... **(818) 449-3106**
180 South Lake Avenue Suite 335, Pasadena, CA 91101
*Travel agency that specializes in freighter travel.*

## PASSPORTS

If you do not have a valid U.S. passport you will need to apply for one a couple of months prior to your trip. Foreigners must have a current passport from their country. A U.S. passport is valid for ten years. The current charge is $65. The fee is lower if you deal directly with one of the thirteen passport agencies listed on the next page.

It is possible to get your passport in one day; however, you must be able to show that you are leaving the country in less than seventy-two hours. This will be very difficult to do if you are traveling as a courier. For an additional charge you can have your passport in one week. Your best bet is to obtain your passport long before your date of departure. Do not wait until summer as the lines can be extremely long. If you are not located near a passport office, the main post office in your city will provide an application.

You can obtain your passport quicker by going to one of the thirteen Passport Agency Offices listed on the next page.

**Boston Passport Agency** ...................................................... **(617) 565-6990**
10 Causeway Street, Room 247, Thomas P. O'Neil Federal Building, Boston, MA 02222

**Chicago Passport Agency** ................................................... **(312) 341-6020**
Duczynski Federal Building, Room 380, 230 South Dearborn Street, Chicago, IL 60604

**Honolulu Passport Agency** ............................................... **(808) 522-8283**
1132 Bishop Street, Suite 500, Honolulu, HI 96850

**Houston Passport Agency** ................................................. **(713) 209-3160**
1919 Smith Street, Houston, TX 77002

**Los Angeles Passport Agency** ........................................ **No calls please**
Federal Building, 11000 Wilshire Boulevard, Room 13100, Los Angeles, CA 90024-3615

**Miami Passport Agency** ...................................................... **(305) 539-3600**
Federal Office Building, 3rd Floor, 51 SW First Avenue, Miami, FL 33130

**New Orleans Passport Agency** .......................................... **(504) 589-6161**
Postal Services Building, 12th Floor, 701 Loyola Avenue, New Orleans, LA 70113

**New York Passport Agency** .............................................. **No calls please**
376 Hudson Street, New York, NY 10014

**Philadelphia Passport Agency** .......................................... **(215) 597-7480**
United States Custom House, 200 Chestnut Street, Room 103, Philadelphia, PA 19106

**San Francisco Passport Agency** ...................................... **No calls please**
525 Market Street, San Francisco, CA 94105

**Seattle Passport Agency** .................................................. **(206) 220-7788**
Federal Building, Suite 992, 915 Second Avenue, Seattle, WA 98174

**Stamford Passport Agency** ................................................ **(203) 325-4401**
One Landmark Square, Broad and Atlantic Streets, Stamford, CT 06901

**Washington D.C. Passport Agency** ................................... **(202) 647-0518**
1111 19th Street NW, Washington, DC 20524

## VISAS

A visa is an official approval for you to enter a country. Currently over half of all countries require them. You will need to consult the courier companies, airlines, consulates, or embassies about whether you will need a visa. In order to obtain one, you will have to write directly to the consulate or embassy. Some visas cost money, while others are free.

If you are interested in having someone else do the legwork for you or you are in a rush, there are a couple of companies that, for a fee, offer this service.

**Express Visa Service** ............................................................ **(202) 337-2442**
2150 Wisconsin Avenue, Suite 20, Washington, DC 20007

**Passport Plus** .......................................... **(800) 367-1818 or (212) 759-5540**
20 E 49th Street, Third Floor, New York, NY 10017

## HOSTELS AND HOTELS

Youth hostels are a wonderful way to avoid costly hotel bills and meet many interesting people. Hostels are not like hotels. Each hostel has its own individuality, but common customs pervade. They all have dormitory-style sleeping quarters and bathroom facilities separated for males and females. The rooms are furnished with bunk beds, mattresses, pillows, and blankets. Hostels have fully equipped self-service kitchens, dining rooms, and common rooms. Under the supervision of a residential manager, most hostels have a curfew at night. Hostellers may be asked to help with a small task to contribute to the hostel's upkeep, and are responsible for cleaning up after themselves. Environmental recycling practices are employed as well as a smoke-free policy. Alcohol and illegal drugs are not permitted.

Hostelling International–American Youth Hostels (HI–AYH) is a nonprofit membership organization founded in 1934 to promote international understanding by educational travel through an operating network of 6,000 hostels in 70 countries.

The mission of AYH is "To help all people, especially young people, gain a greater understanding of the world and its people." AYH is comprised of 38 local councils, each responsible for its own development, maintenance, operation, and fund-raising.

There are over 3,000 youth hostels in Europe, and over 200 in the United States. The average cost for a night is $3–$20 in Europe and $7–$30 in the United States. For more information contact an organization in the following list:

**American Youth Hostel**............................................................ **(202) 737-5537**
1009 11th Street NW, Washington, DC 20001

**Canadian Hostelling Association** ...................................... **(613) 237-7884**
400-205 Catherine Street, Ottawa, ON K2P 1C3

**YHA England and Wales** .............................................. **(441) (71) 836-8541**
14 Southampton Street, London WC2E 7HY, England

## INTERNATIONAL HOSTEL DIRECTORY

The following is a list of some inexpensive places to sleep either in the departure cities for your courier flights or just when visiting these great cities.

## AMSTERDAM

**Access International, Ltd.** ...................................................... **(800) 825-3633**

**Frisco Inn** .......................................................................... **(31) (20) 620-1610**
Beurst. 5, Amsterdam
*f35 per person per night*

**Hotel Casa Cara** ............................................................... **(31) (20) 662-3135**
Emmast. 24, Amsterdam
*f70–95 single / f130 double per night*

**'t Ancker** ........................................................................... **(31) (20) 662-9560**
De Ruijterkade 100, Amsterdam
*Located near central station*
*f40 for dorm room per night*

## ATHENS

**Acropolis House** .................................................. **(30) (1) 322-2344**
Voulis Kodrou 6 Street, Athens
*Very elegant hotel*
*13,000GDR single (including breakfast) / 15,590GDR double (including breakfast)*

**Athens International Youth Hostel** .............................. **(30) (1) 523-4170**
16 Victor Hugo Street, Athens
*1,500GDR per night*
*2,100GDR for non-members, includes membership card*

**Pella Inn** .......................................................... **(30) (1) 325-0598**
104 Ermou Street, Athens
*Popular hotel with balcony rooms that have a great view of the Acropolis*
*4,000GDR single / 6,000GDR double / 7,500GDR triple*

## BANGKOK

**Bangkok International Youth Hostel** .......................... **(66) (2) 281-0361**
25/2 Phitsanulok Road, Sisao Theves, Dusit, Bangkok 10300
*250 Baht per night*

## BARCELONA

**Marc de deu de Montserrat** .................................... **(34) (3) 210-5151**
Passeig Marc de Deu del Coll 41-51, CP 08023 Barcelona
*1,700Ptas per night for members*
*Membership cards are sold here*
*Only those under the age of 25 may stay here*

**Hostal de Joves** ................................................. **(34) (3) 300-3104**
Passeig Pujades 29, CP 08018 Barcelona
*1,500Ptas per night per person under the age of 25*
*1,700Ptas per night per person over the age of 25*
*Breakfast is included*

**Pere Tarres** ...................................................... **(34) (3) 410-2309**
Numancia 149, CP 08029 Barcelona
*1,400Ptas per night per person*
*Breakfast is included*

Studio ........................................................................... (34) (3) 205-0961
Duquesa d'Orleans 58, CP 08034 Barcelona
*1,450Ptas per night*
*This hostel is open only for the summer (June–August)*

## Boston

Boston International Youth Hostel ..................................... (617) 536-9455

General info line ................................................................. (617) 731-5430
12 Hemingway, Boston, MA 02115
*$18 per night for members*
*$21 per night for non-members*

## Brussels

Jacques Brel ........................................................................ (32) (2) 218-0187
Rue de la Sablonniere 30, 1000 Bruxelles
*395BF per night for a dormitory room*
*450BF per night for a room with four people*
*616BF per night for a single*

Bruegel ............................................................................... (32) (2) 511-0436
1000 Brussel, Heilig Geestraat 2
*395BF per night for a dormitory room (995BF for non-members)*
*450BF per night for a room with four people (550BF for non-members)*
*660BF per night for a single (760BF for non-members)*

## Chicago

Chicago Summer Hostel ...................................................... (773) 327-5350
731 S Plymouth Court, Chicago, IL 60605
*$21 per night for members / $36 per night for non-members*
*(closed September 3–June 7)*

International House of Chicago ......................................... (773) 753-2270
1414 E 59th Street, Chicago, IL 60637
*$21 per night for members / $36 per night for non-members*
*Single room accommodations*

# WHAT IS A HOSTEL, ANYWAY?

- *Hostels offer unbeatable savings on overnight lodging. Enjoy a dormitory-style bedroom and shared bathroom for around $8–$16 per night, plus global discounts on car rentals, sports equipment, museum admissions, meals, and more!*

- *Hostels provide separate sleeping quarters for males and females. Some provide private family rooms. Beds come with blankets and pillows, while hostellers provide (or Rent) their own towels and linens.*

- *Most hostels provide fully-equipped, self-service kitchens. Some have laundry facilities, libraries, hot tubs, private rooms for couples and families, concierge services, and other amenities.*

- *The most extensive network of hostels is organized by the International Youth Hostel Federation. An AYH membership card provides access to all 6,000 IYHF hostels in 70 countries around the world.*

- *Hostelling International is the new seal of approval of the International Youth Hostel Federation.*

- *Hostels are set in strikingly beautiful castles, in ultra-modern facilities near urban centers, or in tranquil rural settings.*

- *Hostels are open to travelers of all ages, except in the Bavarian region of Germany, where the age limit is 26.*

- *The* Guide to Budget Accommodations *provides up-to-date listings on all hostels. Volume 1 covers Europe and the Mediterranean region. Volume 2 covers the rest of the world. Both books are available from AYH council offices across the nation.*

- *AYH membership is valid for twelve months from the date of issue and includes a free copy of* Hosteling in North America: A guide to Hostels in Canada and the U.S.A.

## COPENHAGEN

**Amager** ...................................................... **(45) 325 22 908**
Vejlandsalle 200, 2300 Copenhagen S
*$70 for dormitory room; $200 for singles; $300 for four people*
*Rates are for members only.*

**Bellahoj** ......................................................**(45) 382 89 715**
Danhostel Bellahoj, Herbervejen 8, 2700 Bronshoj
*70kr per night for members*
*95 kr per night for non-members*
*Closed during the winter until March 1st*

## DUBAI

**Dubai Hostel** ................................................... **(971) (4) 625 578**
Al Qusais Road, Dubai

## DUBLIN

**Dublin International** ....................................... **(353) (1) 830-1766**
61 Mountjoy Street, Dublin 7
*8L per night for members*
*8.50L per night for non-members*

**Harcourt Street** ................................................. **(353) (1) 475-0430**
Harcourt Street, Dublin 2
*9L per night*

## FRANKFURT

**Haus der Jugend** ................................................. **(49) (69) 619 058**
Deuscherrnufer 12, 60594 Frankfurt
*DM32 per night in a dormitory room*
*DM37.50 for three or four people*
*Members only*

## GUAYAQUIL

**Guayaquil Youth Hostel** ................................... **(593) (4) 248 357**
Ecuahogar, Av Isidro Ayora (Sauces I), Frente al Banco Ecuatoriano de
la Vivienda MZF31V20, Guayaquil

## HONG KONG

**Bradbury Hall** ...................................................... (852) 232 82 458
Check Keng, Sai Kung Peninsula, New Territories

**Ma Wui Hall** ........................................................ (852) 281 75 715
Top of Mt. Davis Path, off Victoria Road, Kennedy Town, Hong Kong
Island
*HK$55 for members*
*HK$95 for non-members*

**Jockey Club Mong Tung Wan Youth Hostel** .................. (852) 298 41 389
Lantau Island
*HK$25 for members*
*HK$50 for non-members*

**S. G. Davis Youth Hostel** ...................................... (852) 298 55 610
Ngong Ping, Lantau Island
*HK$35 for members*
*HK$65 for non-members*

**Hoi Ha Youth Hostel** ............................................ (852) 232 82 327
Hoi Ha Road, Pak Sah O, Sai Kung Peninsula
*HK$25 per night*

**Bradbury Lodge** .................................................. (852) 266 25 123
Off Ting Kok Road, Tai Mei Tuk, Tai Po, New Territories
*HK$45 per night*

**Sze Lok Yuen Hostel** ............................................ (852) 248 88 188
Off Tai Mo Shan Road, Tsuen Wan, New Territories

## JOHANNESBURG

**Fairview Hostel** ................................................. (27) (11) 618-2048
4 College Street, Fairview 2094, Johannesburg
*R35 per night for a shared room; R50 per night for a private room*

**Johannesburg Central Hostel** ................................. (27) (11) 643-1213
4 Fife Avenue, Berea, Johannesburg
*R25 per night for members*
*R28 per night for non-members*

**Kew Hostel** ....................................................... (27) (11) 887-9072
5 Johannesburg Road, Kew 2090, Johannesburg
*R35 per night*

**Rockey Street Backpackers** ........................................... **(27) (11) 648-8786**
34 Regent Street, Yeoville, Johannesburg
  *R35 for a dorm; R65 for a single; R95 for a double; R110 for a deluxe room*

**Dunkeld West, The Backpackers' Ritz** ....................... **(27) (11) 792-1376**
6 North Road, Dunkeld West, Johannesburg
  *R35 per night*

**The Pink House**............................................................. **(27) (11) 487-1991**
Becker Street, Yeoville, Johannesburg 2192

## Kuala Lumpur

**Kuala Lumpur International Youth Hostel**.................. **(60) (3) 273-6870**
21 Jalan Kampung Attap, 50460 Kuala Lumpur

## Lisbon

**Pousada de Juventude de Lisboa**................................. **(351) (1) 353-2696**
Rua Andrade Corvo 46, 1000 Lisboa
  *$2340 per night*

**Catalazete** ........................................................................ **(351) (1) 443-0638**
Estrada Marginal, 2780 Oerias
  *$1500 per night*

## Los Angeles

**Colonial Inn Youth Hostel** ................................................ **(714) 536-3315**
421 Eighth Street, Huntington Beach, CA 92648
  *Centrally located near Disneyland and beaches*
  *$14 per person for a bunk room; $16 per person for a double room*

**Fullerton Youth Hostel** ......................................................... **(714) 738-3721**
1700 North Harbor Boulevard, Fullerton, CA 92635
  *$13.75 per night for members*
  *$16.75 per night for non-members*

**Los Angeles South Bay Youth Hostel** .............................. **(310) 831-8109**
3601 S Gaffey Street, #613, San Pedro, CA 90733
  *$20.16 per night in a dorm room for members*
  *$23.16 per night in a dorm room for non-members*

**Santa Monica International AYH-Hostel** ........................ **(310) 393-9913**
1436 Second Street, Santa Monica, CA 90401
*$17.92 per night for members*
*See Spotlight*

## LONDON

**Hampstead Heath Youth Hostel** ................................ **(441) (81) 458-9054**
4 Wellgarth Road, Golders Green, London NW11 7HR
*See Spotlight*

### Santa Monica International AYH-Hostel
### (310) 393-9913
1436 Second Street, Santa Monica, CA 90401
$17.92 per night for members

*The Santa Monica hostel is a great base for those wishing to explore the Los Angeles area without a car. Convenient to shopping, cafes, restaurants, movie theaters, and just two blocks from the beach, this is a great hostel for those who like to have fun. There are regularly-scheduled trips to Disneyland and Universal Studios, and the J. Paul Getty Museum is just a bus ride away.*

**HOSTEL SPOTLIGHT**

Ken Geser, American Youth Hostels

**Regency House Hotel**.....................................................(441) (71) 637-1804
71 Gower Street, London
*Extremely charming bed & breakfast with personable owner*
*£35 for a single; £45 for a double*

**Rotherhithe Youth Hostel** .........................................(441) (71) 232-2114
Salter Road, London SE16 1PP
*An ultra-modern building with every facility for groups and individual*
*travelers alike, including meeting and conference facilities*
*£20.50 for a dorm room; £23.50 for a double*

**Swiss House Hotel** ........................................................(441) (71) 373-2769
171 Old Brompton Road, South Kensington, London
*Close to most of London's main attractions*
*Winner of the Best Value Bed & Breakfast Award*
*£56 for a single; £72 for a double*

## MADRID

**Albergue Juvenil (IYHF)** ...................................................(34) (1) 547-4532
Calle Sta Cruz de Marcenado No 28, Madrid
*950ptas per night*

## MANCHESTER

**Potato Wharf** ....................................................................(44) (161) 839-9960
Castlefield, Manchester M3 4MB
*11.5L per person for a six-person room*
*13L per person for a four-person room*
*Add 1.70L for non-members; after six nights, non-members get member*
*rates.*

## MANILA

**Manila International Youth Hostel** ...............................(63) (2) 832-0680
4227 Palmas Street, Claudio, Paranaque
*100p per night for members*
*130p for non-members*

## MELBOURNE

**Queensberry Hill International Hostel** ...................... **(61) (3) 932 98 599**
78 Howard Street, North Melbourne, Victoria 3051
  *Dorm rooms are A$17 per night for members.*
  *Dorm rooms are A$20 per night for non-members.*
  *Single rooms are A$45 per night for members.*
  *Single rooms are A$48 per night for non-members.*

## Hampstead Heath Youth Hostel (441) (81) 458-9054

*4 Wellbarth Road, Golders Green,*
*London NW11 7HR*
*From £15.60 per night for members*

    *This two-hundred-bed hostel located near the Hippodrome is one of seven official AYH hostels located in London. With reasonable rates, this 'round-the-clock hostel is a great place to stay for those who want to be in London but away from the crowded city center. A dorm room is available for £15.60 per night, a four-person room for £18.55, and a single for £37. Add £1.70 for non-members.*

**HOSTEL SPOTLIGHT**

Jim Kennett, American Youth Hostels

## MIAMI

**Miami Beach International AYH-Hostel** ........................ **(305) 534-2988**
1438 Washington Avenue, Miami Beach, FL 33139
*Rooms with a shared bath are $14. Rooms with a private bath are $45 for*
*one person or $49.50 for two.*
*See Spotlight*

**Miami Beach International Travelers Hostel** ................. **(305) 534-0268**
236 Ninth Street, Miami Beach, FL 33139
*Budget accommodations for the international traveler*

## MILAN

**Piero Rotta** ...................................................................... **(39) (2) 392 67 095**
Via martino Bassi 2 (QT8-San Siro), 20148 Milano
*This hostel is open from December 23 to January 13.*
*24,000L per night for a six-person room*

## MONTREAL

**Auberge de Montrea** .......................................................... **(514) 843-3317**
1030, Mackey Street, Montreal, Quebec H3G 2HI
*$17.50 per night for members*
*$22 per night for non-members*
*$1.75 to rent bedding*

## MUNICH

**Pension Clara** .................................................................. **(49) (89) 348 374**
25 Wilhelmstrasse, Munich
*DM60 single / DM85 double*

**Pension Frank** ................................................................. **(49) (89) 281 451**
24 Schellingstrasse, Munich
*Popular with backpackers*
*DM55 single / DM85 double*
*Breakfast is included*

**Thalkirchen Jugendgastehaus** ..................................... **(49) (89) 723-6550**
Meisingstrasse 4, 81379 Munich
*DM35 for a single / DM31.50 per person for a double*

## NAIROBI

**Nairobi Youth Hostel** ......................................................... **(254) (2) 721 765**
Ralph Bunche Road, P.O. Box 48661, Nairobi

---

### Miami Beach International AYH-Hostel (305) 534-2988

*1438 Washington Avenue,*
*Miami Beach, FL 33139*
*From $14 per night for members*

*The Miami Beach International Hostel is in the heart of the Old Miami Beach Art Deco District, which is listed on the National Register of Historic Places. In its early days, the building was a hangout for Al Capone's legendary gambling syndicate. The hostel is only two blocks from the beach and within easy walking distance of ethnic restaurants, nightclubs, and boutiques that give Miami Beach a Latin sizzle. This is where I stay when in Miami Beach. A room with a shared bath is $14, a single is $45, and a double is $49.50.*

**HOSTEL SPOTLIGHT**

American Youth Hostels

## NEW YORK

**Allerton House** ................................................. **(212) 753-8841**
130 East 57th Street, New York, NY 10022
*Women only*
*$55 per night / $85 per night with bathroom*

**New York International AYH Hostel** .............................. **(212) 932-2300**
891 Amsterdam Avenue (W 103rd Street), New York, NY 10025
*$20 per night for members / $23 per night for non-members*
*See Spotlight*

**The Gershwin** ..................................................... **(212) 545-8000**
7 East 27th, New York, NY 10016
*$22 per night for dormitory accomodations*
*$60–99 per night for a private room including bathroom and television*

## OSAKA

**Hattori Ryokuchi Youth Hostel** ...................................... **(81) (6) 862-0600**
1-3 Hattori-ryokuchi, Toyonaka-shi, Osaka-fu 560
*¥1,800 per night*

## PARIS

**Arpajon** .......................................................... **(33) (1) 649 02 885**
3 rue Marcel Duhamel, 91290 Arpajon
*46F per night*

**Cite des Sciences** ............................................... **(33) (1) 484 32 411**
24, rue des Sept Arpents, 93310 Le Pre St Gervais
*113F per night*

**Clichy "Leo Lagrange"** ......................................... **(33) (1) 412 72 690**
107 rue Martre, 92110 Clichy
*171F per night for a single*
*128F per person for a double*

**Jules Ferry** ..................................................... **(33) (1) 435 75 560**
8 Boulevard Jules Ferry, 75011 Paris
*113F per night*

**Le d'Artagnan** ................................................... **(33) (1) 403 23 453**
80 rue Vitruve, 75020 Paris
*113F per night*

**Relais Europeen Athismons** ......................................... **(33) (1) 698 48 139**
Relais Europeen de la Jeuness, 52 avenue Robert Schumann, 91200 Athis
Mons (Essonne)
*85F per night*

**3 Ducks Hostel** ................................................................ **(33) (1) 484 20 405**
6 pl. E Pernet, Paris
*87F for dormitory housing / 107F per person for a double*

**Y & H Hostel** .................................................................... **(33) (1) 453 50 953**
80 rue Mouffetard, Paris
*Great location and friendly atmosphere*
*97F per night per person in a dorm*
*117F per person for a double room*

## PHILADELPHIA

**Bank Street Hostel** ............................... **(800) 392-4678 or (215) 922-0222**
32 S Bank Street, Philadelphia, PA 19106
*$16 per night for members*
*$19 per night for non-members*

**Chamounix Mansion** .......................................................... **(215) 878-3676**
West Fairmount Park, Philadelphia, PA 19131
*$11 per night for men*
*$14 per night for women*

## QUITO

**Hostelling International Quito** ........................................ **(593) (2) 543 995**
Pinto 385 y Reina Victoria, near Amazonas Avenue, Quito, Ecuador
*$9 per night*

## RIO DE JANEIRO

**Rio de Janeiro Youth Hostel** ......................................... **(55) (21) 286-0303**
Rua General Dionisio 63, Botafogo, 22271-050 Rio de Janeiro, RJ
*160 centavos per night*

**Copacabana Praia Youth Hostel** .................................... **(55) (21) 236-6472**
Rua Tenente Marones de Gusmao 85, Rio de Janeiro
*The best place for the budget traveler in Rio*
*Very friendly place near the beach*
*Very cheap—$8 single*

**Hotel Benjamin Constant**
Rua Benjamin Constant 10, Rio de Janeiro
*One of the cheapest places to stay in Rio*
*Rooms are small and dingy*
*$3 single*

## New York International AYH-Hostel (212) 932-2300

*891 Amsterdam Avenue (West 103rd Street),*
*New York, NY 10025*
*From $20 per night for members*

*From museums to theaters, from skyscrapers to historic neighborhoods, New York City has it all. The New York International AYH-Hostel is in a landmark Victorian Gothic-style building on the city's bustling Upper West Side. Near Central Park and Columbia University, the hostel offers a lively program of walking tours, a hospitality desk staffed by neighborhood volunteers, group outings to concerts and sporting events, and discounts or free tickets to off-Broadway shows, comedy clubs, concerts, and other events. Expect to pay $20 per night for members, $23 for non-members.*

**HOSTEL SPOTLIGHT**

American Youth Hostels

**Hotel Ferreira Viana** ........................................................(55) (21) 205-7396
Rua Ferreira Viana 58, Rio de Janeiro
*Very cheap rooms*
*$13.50 single / $27 double*

**Hotel Turistico** ................................................................(55) (21) 225-9388
Ladeira da Gloria 30, Rio de Janeiro
*Very popular safe and clean budget hotel with foreigners*
*$9 single with balcony*

## ROME

**'Foro Italico** .......................................................(39) (6) 323-6267
A F Pessina', Viale delle olimpiadi 61, 00194 Rome
*L23,000 per night*

**Pensione Papa Germano** ...................................................(39) (6) 486 919
14a Calatafimi, Rome
*L50,000 per night for a single*
*L70,000 per night for a double*

## SAN FRANCISCO

**The Essex Hotel** ................ (800) 45-Essex (USA) or (800) 44-Essex (CA)
684 Ellis Street, San Francisco, CA 94109
*An excellent choice for quality accommodations and an unbeatable price of*
*$59 per night for single / $69 per night for double. Centrally located, it is an*
*ideal starting point for San Francisco sightseeing.*

**San Francisco AYH Downtown** .......................................... (415) 788-5604
312 Mason Street, San Francisco, CA 94102
*$16 per night for members*
*$19 per night for non-members*

**San Francisco International Hostel** ................................... (415) 771-7277
240 Fort Mason, San Francisco, CA 94123
*$16 per night*
*See Spotlight*

**San Francisco International Student Center** ................... (415) 255-8800
1188 Folsom Street, San Francisco, CA 94103
*$13 per night*

## SANTIAGO

**Hostelling International Santiago** ..................................(56) (2) 671-8532
Cienfuegos 151, Santiago de Chile
*4,000 pesos per night for members*
*5,500 pesos per night for non-members*

### San Francisco International Hostel (415) 771-7277

*240 Fort Mason, San Francisco, CA 94123*
*$16 per night*

*Ah, San Francisco! Cable cars climbing steep fog-shrouded hills and the famous Golden Gate Bridge make the "City by the Bay" one of America's most intriguing and popular distinations. The San Francisco International AYH-Hostel is located at Fort Mason in the Golden Gate National Recreation Area, an urban national park right on the bay. Fort Mason is also home to museums, galleries, and theaters. Fisherman's Wharf, Chinatown, and Ghiradelli Square are all within easy walking distance. This hostel is often booked, especially in summer.*

**HOSTEL SPOTLIGHT**

Ellen Davis, American Youth Hostels

## SAO PAULO

**Bela Vista** .......................................................... **(55) (11) 607-3662**
Rua Joao Passalacqua 181, Bela Vista, SP

**Magdalena Tagliaferro** .................................................. **(55) (11) 605-3077**
Estada Turitica do Jaragua 651,
Pargque Estadual do Jaragua, 05161-0000, Sao Paulo, SP

## SEATTLE

**Seattle International Youth Hostel** ..................................... **(206) 622-5443**
84 Union Street, Seattle, WA 98101
*$17 per night for members*
*$20 per night for non-members*

## SEOUL

**Seoul Olympic** .................................................................. **(82) (2) 410-2114**
Olympic YH, 88 Bangyi-Dong, Songpa-Ku, Seoul 138-749
*W11,100 per night for members*

## SINGAPORE

**Hotel Asia** ............................................................. **(65) 737-8388**
37 Scotts Road, Singapore
*Modest economy hotel*
*Rooms have air-conditioning*
*S$118 for a single room*

**Metropole Hotel** ....................................................... **(65) 336-3611**
41 Seah Street, Singapore
*54-room modest hotel*
*Rooms have air-conditioning and TV*
*S$105.50 per night for a standard single room*

**Metropolitan YMCA, Tanglin Centre** ................................ **(65) 737-7755**
60 Stevens Road, Singapore
*Large YMCA with pool, gym, squash courts, cheap rooms, and food*
*S$91 per person per night*

## STOCKHOLM

**af Chapman/Skeppsholmen** ............................................. (46) (8) 679-5015
Vandrarhem 'af Chapman', Skeppsholmen, 11149 Stockholm
  *130 SEK per night for members; 170 SEK for non-members*

**Skeppsholmen Vastra Bröbanken** ................................ (46) (8) 679-5017
Vandrarhem, Skeppsholmen Vastra Bröbanken, 11149 Stockholm
  *100 SEK per night for members*
  *135 SEK per night for non-members*

**Backpackers Inn** ............................................................... (46) (8) 660-7515
Banergatan 56, Box 9116, 10272 Stockholm
  *Open from the end of June to the middle of August*

**Zinken** ............................................................................... (46) (8) 616-8100
**After hours number** ....................................................... (46) (8) 616-8188
Vandrarhem Zinken, Zinkensvag 20, 11741 Stockholm
  *170 SEK per night*

**Langholmen** .................................................................... (46) (8) 668-0510
Vandrarhem Langholmen, Kronohaktet, Box 9116, 10272 Stockholm
  *125 SEK per night for members*
  *160 SEK per night for non-members*

## SYDNEY

**Challis Lodge** .................................................................. (61) (2) 358-5422
21-23 Challis Avenue, Potts Point, Sydney 2011
  *62 rooms in huge pink Victorian mansion*
  *Very clean and inexpensive*
  *A$32 per night with shared bath / A$42 with private bath*

**Glebe Point** ..................................................................... (61) (2) 692-8418
262 Glebe Point Road, Glebe, New South Wales 2037
  *A$18 per night for members*
  *A$20 for non-members*

**Hereford Lodge** .............................................................. (61) (2) 660-5577
51 Hereford Street, Glebe, New South Wales 2037
  *A$19 per night for members*
  *A$21 per night for non-members*

**Waratah Central** .............................................................. (61) (2) 281-8333
22-44 Albion Street, Surry Hills, Sydney
  *182 spacious rooms in this moderately priced hotel*
  *Large pool*

## TEL AVIV

**Tel Aviv Youth Hostel** ....................................................**(972) (3) 544-1748**
36 Bnei Dan Street, Tel Aviv 62260
*$25 (US currency) per night for a dormitory room*
*$38 (US currency) per night for a single*

## TOKYO

**Japan YWCA Hostel** ........................................................ **(81) (3) 326 87 313**
3-1-1 Shinjuku Ichigawa, Sabowara, Tokyo
*11 room hostel*
*Very inexpensive*
*Women only*
*¥6,000 per night*

**Tokyo International Youth Hostel** ............................... **(81) (3) 323 51 107**
21-1 Kagura-kashi, Shinjuku-ku, Tokyo
*138 bed hostel*
*¥2,900 per night*

**Tokyo YMCA** ................................................................. **(81) (3) 329 31 919**
7 Mitoshirocho Kanda, Chiyoda-ku, Tokyo
*86 room hostel*
*¥11,330 per night*

**Yoyogi Youth Hostel** .....................................................**(81) (3) 346 79-163**
National Olympics Memorial Youth Center, 31 Yoyogi Kami-zono-cho,
Shibuya-ku, Tokyo 151

## TORONTO

**Hostelling International Toronto**........ **(800) 668-4487 or (416) 971-4440**
223 Church Street, Toronto, Ontario, Canada M5B 1Y7
*$18.95 per night for members*
*$22.95 per night for non-members*
*Dormitory housing*

## VANCOUVER

**Vancouver Jericho Beach** ..................................................... **(604) 224-3208**
1515 Discovery Street (Jericho Park), Vancouver, BC, Canada V6R 4K5
*$16 per night for members*
*$20 per night for non-members*

## VIENNA

**Myrthengasse (IYHF)**
1070 Myrthengasse 7, Neustiftgasse 85, Vienna
*130AS per person*
*Members only*

**Jungendherberg Lechnerstrasse**
Wien, Lechnerstrasse 12

**Jungendgastehaus Wein**
Brigittenau, 1200 Wien, Friedrich Engelsplatz 24, Vienna

**Jungendgastehaus der Stadt Wien**
Hutteldorf, Schlossberggasse 8

**Hostel Ruthensteiner**
Ruthensteiner JH, 1150 Wien, Robert Hameulinggasse 24

## WASHINGTON D.C.

**Hostelling International Washington, DC** ...................... **(202) 737-2333**
1009 11th Street NW, Washington DC 20001
*$18 per night for members*
*$21 per night for non-members*

## ZURICH

**Wollishofen** ........................................................................**(41) (1) 482-3544**
Mutschellenstrasse 114, Zurich
*Busy hostel but very clean*
*29Fr for members / 34Fr for non-members*
*80Fr member price for singles*

**Marthahaus** ........................................................................**(41) (1) 251-4550**
36 Zahringerstrasse, Zurich
*Dorm rooms for 65Fr single / 104Fr double/146Fr triple*

# HI-AYH COUNCILS ACROSS THE UNITED STATES

The following is a list of youth hostel council offices throughout the country, where travelers can stock up on information helpful for planning a trip. Council offices sell IYH memberships and hostel directories, and keep a supply of travel-related books and brochures on hand for visitors.

## ALASKA

**Alaska Council** ...................................................................... **(907) 562-7772**
700 H Street, Anchorage, AK 99501

## ARIZONA

**Arizona-Southern Nevada Council** .................................. **(520) 774-2731**
23 N Laroux, Flagstaff, AZ 86001

## CALIFORNIA

**Golden Gate Council** ........................................................... **(415) 863-1444**
425 Divisadero Street, #307, San Francisco, CA 94117

**Los Angeles Council** ............................................................ **(310) 393-6263**
1434 Second Street, Santa Monica, CA 90401

**San Diego Council** ................................................................ **(619) 338-9981**
655 Fourth Avenue Suite 45, San Diego, CA 92101

## COLORADO

**Rocky Mountain Council** ..................................................... **(303) 442-1166**
1310 College Avenue Suite 315, Boulder, CO 80306

## CONNECTICUT

**Council Office Yankee Council** .......................................... **(203) 247-6356**
118 Oak Street, Hartford, CT 06106

## DISTRICT OF COLUMBIA

Potomac Area Council ........................................................ (202) 783-0717
1108 K Street NW 2nd Floor, Washington, DC 20005

## FLORIDA

Florida Council ................................................................. No calls please
13819 G Walsingham Road #223, Largo, FL 34644

## GEORGIA

Georgia Council .................................................................. (404) 872-8844
P.O. Box 87477, Atlanta, GA 30337

## HAWAII

c/o National Office ............................................................ (202) 783-6161
733 15th Street NW Suite 840, Washington, DC 20005

## IDAHO

Oregon Council .................................................................. (503) 236-3380
3031 Hawthorne Boulevard SE, Portland, OR 97214

## ILLINOIS

Metropolitan Chicago Council ........................................... (312) 327-8114
2232 West Roscoe, Chicago, IL 60618

## INDIANA

Indiana Council ................................................................. (317) 844-5320
1010 East 86th Street Suite 34-E, Indianapolis, IN 46230

## Iowa

**Northeast Iowa Council** ...................................................... **(319) 864-3923**
P.O. Box 10, Postville, IA 52162

## Louisiana

**c/o HI-AYH National Office** ............................................... **(202) 783-6161**
733 15th Street NW Suite 840, Washington, DC 20005

## Maine

**Eastern New England Council** ........................................... **(617) 731-6692**
1020 Commonwealth Avenue, Boston, MA 02215

## Maryland

**Potomac Area Council** ....................................................... **(202) 783-0717**
1108 K Street NW 2nd Floor, Washington, DC 20005

## Massachusetts

**Greater Boston Council** ..................................................... **(617) 731-5430**
1020 Commonwealth Avenue, Boston, MA 02215

## Michigan

**Michigan Council** ............................................................... **(248) 545-0511**
3024 Coolidge, Berkley, MI 48072

## Minnesota

**Minnesota Council** ............................................................ **(612) 378-3773**
125 SE Main Street, Suite 235, Minneapolis, MN 55417

## MONTANA

c/o HI-AYH National Office ................................................ (202) 783-6161
733 15th Street NW Suite 840, Washington, DC 20005

## NEBRASKA

Nebraskaland Council ........................................................ (402) 472-5358
P.O. Box 880221, Lincoln, NE 68501

## NEW HAMPSHIRE

Eastern New England Council ........................................... (617) 731-6692
1020 Commonwealth Avenue, Boston, MA 02215

## NEW JERSEY

Delaware Valley Council .................................................... (215) 925-6004
624 South Third Street, Philadelphia, PA 19147

## NEW MEXICO

New Mexico Council ........................................................... (505) 867-6596
PO Box 4177, Albuquerque, NM 87196

## NEW YORK

Niagara Frontier Council ................................................... (716) 852-5222
667 Main Street, P.O. Box 1110, Buffalo, NY 14205
  *Please send mail only to the P.O Box address.*

Syracuse Council ................................................................ (315) 472-5788
535 Oak Street, Syracuse, NY 13203

Hudson-Mohawk Council .................................................. (518) 472-1914
P.O. Box 7066, Albany, NY 12225

## NORTH CAROLINA

**Piedmont Council** ................................................................. **(919) 454-5027**
P.O. Box 10766, Winston-Salem, NC 27108

**Coastal Carolina Council** ..................................................... **(910) 661-0444**
173 NE Broad Street, Southern Pines, NC 28387

## OHIO

**Cincinnati Tri-State Council** ............................................... **(513) 651-1294**
PO Box 141015, Cincinnati, OH 45250-1015

**Lima Council Office** ............................................................ **(419) 222-7301**
PO Box 173, Lima, OH 45802

**Northeast Ohio Council** ...................................................... **(216) 467-8711**
6093 Sanford Road, Peninsula, OH 44624

**Toledo Area Council** ............................................................ **(419) 841-4510**
P.O. Box 352736, Toledo, OH 43635-2736

## OREGON

**Oregon Council** .................................................................... **(503) 236-3380**
3031 SE Hawthorne Boulevard, Portland, OR 97214

## PENNSYLVANIA

**Delaware Valley Council** ...................................................... **(215) 925-6004**
624 S Third Street, Philadelphia, PA 19147

**Pittsburgh Council** .............................................................. **(412) 362 8181**
830 East Warrington Avenue, Pittsburgh, PA 15210

## SOUTH DAKOTA

**c/o HI-AYH National Office** ................................................. **(202) 783-6161**
733 15th Street NW Suite 840, Washington, DC 20005

## TENNESSEE

**c/o HI-AYH National Office** ............................................... **(202) 783-6161**
733 15th Street NW Suite 840, Washington, DC 20005

## TEXAS

**Bluebonnet Council** ...................................................... **(713) 520-5332**
2715 Bissonnet, #213, Houston, TX 77005

**North Texas Council** ..................................................... **(214) 350-4294**
3530 Forset Lane, #127, Dallas, TX 75234

**Southwest Texas Council** .............................................. **(512) 444-2300**
2200 S Lakeshore Boulevard, Austin, TX 78741

## VERMONT

**Yankee Council** ............................................................. **(860) 236-2027**
131 Tremont Street, Hartford, CT 06105

## VIRGINIA

**Potomac Area Council** .................................................. **(202) 783-4943**
1108 K Street NW Lower Level, Washington, DC 20005

## WASHINGTON

**Washington State Council** ............................................. **(206) 281-7306**
419 Queen Anne Avenue N, #101, Seattle, WA 98109

## WISCONSIN

**Wisconsin Council** ........................................................ **(414) 961-2525**
5900 N Port Washington Road, Suite 146, Milwaukee, WI 53217

## WORLDWIDE HOSTS

Servas is yet another option for lodging. Servas is an international organization that joins together hosts and travelers. There are members all over the world. As a traveler you will stay for free in the home of a host. It is an opportunity for both of you to learn about each other's culture. There is an application process, interview, and screening. For an application contact:

**U.S. Servas Committee**
11 John Street, Room 407, New York, NY 10038 ................ (212) 267-0252

## INTERNATIONAL TOURIST OFFICES

The following offices will help you with your trip by providing valuable information about their countries. This information includes maps, lodging, exchange rates, sights, and more. Their services are free.

**Austrian National Tourist Office**
P.O. Box 1142, Times Square, New York, NY 10108-1142 . (212) 944-6880
1010 Oest rue Sherbrooke Suite 1410,
  Montreal, PQ  H3A 2R7 ...................................................... (514) 849-3709

**Brazilian Tourist Travel Agency**
16 West 46th Street, 2nd Floor, New York, NY 10036 ....... (212) 730-1010

**British Tourist Authority**
551 5th Avenue, New York, NY 10176 ............................... (800) 462-2748

**Scandinavian Tourist Board**
655 3rd Avenue, New York, NY 10017 ............................... (212) 949-2333

**European Travel Commission**
1 Rockefeller Plaza Suite 214, New York, NY 10020 ......... (212) 218-1200

**French Government Tourist Office**
444 Madison Avenue Suite 164, New York, NY 10022 ..... (212) 838-7800
676 N Michigan Avenue, Suite 3360, Chicago, IL 60611 ... (312) 751-7800
9454 Wilshire Blvd, Suite 715, Beverly Hills, CA 90212 ... (310) 271-2358
30 St. Patrick Street, Suite 700, Toronto, ON M5G 3A3 .... (416) 593-4723
1981 McGill College Avenue, Montreal, PQ H3A 2W9 .... (514) 288-4264

**German National Tourist Office**
122 E 42nd Street, 52nd Floor, New York, NY 10168 ........ (212) 661-7200
11766 Wilshire Boulevard, Suite 750,
Los Angeles, CA 980025 ..................................................... (310) 575-9799
175 Bloor Street E, North Tower, Suite 604,
Toronto, ON M4W 3R8 ...................................................... (416) 968-1570

**Greek National Tourist Organization**
645 5th Avenue, New York, NY 10022 ............................... (212) 421-5777

**Hong Kong Tourist Association**
590 5th Avenue, New York, NY 10036 ............................... (212) 869-5008

**Irish Tourist Board** ................................................................ (800) 223-6470
345 Park Avenue, New York, NY 10154 ............................. (212) 418-0800

**Japan National Tourist Information**
Rockefeller Center, Suite 1250, New York, NY 10020 ....... (212) 757-5640
165 University Avenue, Toronto, ON M5H 3B8 ................ (416) 366-7140

**Korea National Tourism Corporation**
2 Executive Drive, Suite 750, Fort Lee, NJ 07024 .............. (212) 585-0909

**Mexican Government Tourism Office**
405 Park Avenue, Suite 1401 New York, NY 10022 .......... (212) 755-7261

**Netherlands National Tourist Office** .................. (888) GO HOLLAND
355 Lexington Ave, Suite 1401, New York, NY 10017 ....... (212) 370-7360
225 N Michigan Avenue, Suite 326, Chicago, IL 60601 ..... (312) 819-0300
25 Adelaide Street Suite 710, Toronto, ON M5C 1Y2 ........ (416) 363-1577

**New Zealand Travel Commission**
780 Third Avenue Suite 1904, New York, NY 10017 ......... (212) 832-4038
12400 Wilshire Blvd, Suite 1150, Los Angeles, CA 90025 . (310) 207-1145

**Spanish National Tourist Office** ..................................... (888) OK SPAIN
666 5th Avenue, 35th Floor, New York, NY 10002 ............ (212) 265-8822
845 N Michigan Avenue, Suite 915E, Chicago, IL 60611 .. (312) 642-1992
8383 Wilshire Blvd, Suite 956, Beverly Hill, CA 90211 ..... (213) 658-7188
1221 Brikell Avenue Suite 1850, Miami, FL 33131 ............. (305) 358-1992
112 Bloor Street W, Toronto, ON M58 1M8 ....................... (416) 961-3131

## USEFUL ORGANIZATIONS

**The Center for Global Education** ...................................... **(612) 330-1159**
2211 Riverside Avenue, Box 307, Minneapolis, MN 55454
*Third world tour operator*

**Elderhostel** .......................................................................... **(617) 426-7788**
75 Federal Street, 3rd Floor, Boston, MA 02110-1941
*Study programs in the U.S. and Europe for people over 60*

**Experiment in International Living** ... **(800) 336-1616 or (802) 257-7751**
P.O. Box 676, Battleboro, VT 05302

**Campus Travel** ................................................................**(441) (71) 730-3402**
52 Gosvenor Gardens, London WC1, England

**STA Travel (Student Travel Association)** ......................... **(800) 777-0112**
*Over 100 offices worldwide*

**Travel CUTS (Canadian University Travel Services)** ..... **(416) 979-2406**
187 College Street, Toronto, ON M5T 1P7

**Volunteers for Peace** ........................................................... **(802) 259-2759**
43 Tiffany Road, Belmont, VT 05730

## COUNCIL TRAVEL OFFICES

The Council on International Educational Exchange (CIEE) operates a network of retail travel offices across the country providing low-cost flights, rail passes, language courses, insurance, and books. Call your local council for a free copy of their magazine.

130 E University Drive, Suite A, Tempe, AZ 85281 .......... (602) 966-3544
2486 Channing Way, Berkeley, CA 94704 .......................... (510) 848-8604
UCD, Memorial Union Room 162, Davis, CA 95616 ........ (530) 752-2285
5280 North Jackson, Fresno, CA 93740 ............................... (209) 278-6626
800 North State College Boulevard, Fullerton, CA 92834 ........ No phone
9500 Gilman Dr, Price Center #76, La Jolla, CA 92093 .... (619) 452-0630
1800 Pal Verde Avenue, Suite F, Long Beach, CA 90815 .. (714) 527-7950
10904 Lindbrook Drive, Los Angeles, CA 90024 .............. (310) 208-3551
1020 Westwood Boulevard, Los Angeles, CA 90024 ......... (310) 209-1852
5154 State University Drive, Los Angeles, CA 90032 ............... No phone
18111 Nordhoff Street, Northridge, CA 91330 ........................... No phone
394 University Avenue, Suite 200, Palo Alto, CA 94301 .. (650) 325-3888
54 South Raymond Avenue, Pasadena, CA 91105 ............. (818) 793-5595
743 Fourth Avenue, 1st Floor, San Diego, CA 92101 ......... (619) 544-9632

953 Garnet Avenue, San Diego, CA 92109 ........................ (619) 270-6401
530 Bush Street, San Francisco, CA 94108 ........................ (415) 421-3473
919 Irving Street, Suite 102, San Francisco, CA 94122 ..... (415) 566-6222
903 Embarcadero Del Norte, Isla Vista, CA 93117 ........... (805) 562-8080
1138 13th Street, Boulder, CO 80302 .................................... (303) 447-8101
University Memorial Center Room 164 Campus Box 207
  University of Colorado Boulder, Boulder, CO 80309 ..... (303) 444-3232
900 Auraria Parkway, Suite 203, Denver, CO 80204 ......... (303) 571-0630
320 Elm Street, New Haven CT 06520 .............................. (203) 562-5335
3300 M Street NW, 2nd Floor, Washington, DC 20007 .... (202) 377-6464
1636 West University Avenue, Suite 202,
  Gainesville, FL 32603-1840 ............................................... (352) 371-4455
9100 S Dadeland Blvd, Suite 220, Miami, FL 33156 ......... (305) 670-9261
1561 N Decatur Road, Atlanta, GA 30307 ......................... (404) 377-9997
1153 N Dearborn Street, 2nd Floor, Chicago, IL 60610 .... (312) 951-0585
1634 Orrington Avenue, Evanston, IL 60201 ..................... (847) 475-5070
409 East Fourth Street, Bloomington, IN 47408 ................ (812) 330-1600
2526 Lincoln Say, Ames, IA 50014 ...................................... (515) 296-2326
622 West 12th Street, Lawrence, KS 66044 ......................... (913) 749-3900
6363 St. Charles Avenue, Joseph Danna Center,
  Loyola University, New Orleans, LA 70118 ................... (504) 866-1767
7401 Baltimore Avenue, College Park, MD 20740 ............. (301) 779-1172
44 Main Street, Amherst, MA 01002 .................................... (413) 256-1261
273 Newbury Street, Boston, MA 02116 ............................. (617) 266-1926
12 Eliot St, 2nd Floor, Cambridge, MA 02138 .................... (617) 497-1497
84 Massachusetts Avenue, Cambridge, MA 02139 ........... (617) 225-2555
1220 S University Drive, Suite 208, Ann Arbor, MI 48104 (313) 998-0200
1501 University Ave SE, Suite 300,
  Minneapolis, MN 55414 ................................................... (612) 379-2323
86 Albany Street, New Brunswick, NJ 08901 ..................... (732) 249-6667
206 B Dryden Road, Ithaca, NY 14850 ............................... (607) 277-0373
254 Greene Street, New York, NY 10003 ............................ (212) 254-2525
205 E 42nd Street, New York, NY 10017 ............................. (212) 822-2700
895 Amsterdam Avenue Street, New York, NY 10025 ...... (212) 666-4177
137 E Franklin Street, Suite 106, Chapel Hill, NC 27514 .. (919) 942-2334
8 E 13th Avenue, Columbus, OH 43201 ............................. (614) 294-8696
877 East 13th Street, Eugene, OR 97401 ............................. (541) 344-2263
1222 East 13th Street, EMU Building, Eugene, OR 97403    No phone
1430 SW Park Avenue, Portland, OR 97201 ....................... (503) 228-1900
931 Harrisburg Avenue, Lancaster, PA 17603 ................... (717) 392-8272
3606A Chestnut Steet, Philadelphia, PA 19104 ................. (215) 382-0343
118 Meyran Avenue, Pittsburgh, PA 15213 ........................ (412) 683-1881
220 Calder Way, State College, PA 16801 ........................... (814) 861-3232

220 Thayer Street, Providence, RI 02906 ............................. (401) 331-5810
1641 Cumberland Avenue, Knoxville, TN 37916 .............. (423) 523-9900
2000 Guadalupe Street, Austin, TX 78705 ......................... (512) 472-4931
6715 Hillcrest, Dallas, TX 75205 ......................................... (214) 363-9941
1310 East 200 South, Salt Lake City, UT 84102 ................... (801) 582-5840
1314 NE 43rd Street, Suite 210, Seattle, WA 98105 ........... (206) 632-2448
424 Broadway Avenue E, WA 98102 .................................. (206) 329-4567

## LIST OF RECOMMENDED TRAVEL BOOKS

These books usually can be found at your local bookstore, library, or one of the travel bookstores listed in the next section.

### The Asia Employment Program
*A comprehensive guide to teaching English in Japan, South Korea, Taiwan, Indonesia, Thailand, and China. Available only from ACMedia, P.O. Box 30414, Lansing, MI 48909-7914.*

### The Bed & Breakfast Directory
*This book provides details on over 1,000 B & Bs in the United States and Canada. A handy book when traveling to North America.*

### The Berkeley Guides
*A travel series designed for the budget traveler.*

### The Best Pubs of Great Britain
*One of my favorite books.*

### Birnbaum's Guides
*These books focus on the moderate price range.*

### Cheap Sleeps/Cheap Eats in London
*A great book if you are going to London.*

### Cheap Sleeps/Cheap Eats in Paris
*A great book if you are going to Paris.*

### China Solo: A Guide to Independent Travel in China
*Ideal for courier travelers.*

### The Cruise and Travel Employment Program
*A comprehensive guide to finding employment in the cruise and travel industries. Available only from ACMedia, P.O. Box 30414, Lansing, MI 48909-7914.*

## The Eastern Europe Employment Program
*Another in this series of outstanding employment programs. This guide covers job opportunities primarily teaching English in the Czech and Slovak Republics, Hungary, and Poland. Available from ACMedia, P.O. Box 30414, Lansing, MI 48909-7914.*

## Europe For Free
*A great book with lots of free things to do in Europe.*

## Europe for One: A Complete Guide for Solo Travelers
*Ideal book for courier travelers.*

## Europe: Where the Fun is
*A guide to where the action is in Europe.*

## Fielding's Travel Guides
*Plenty of information in these books, however, much of it is in the expensive range. Look for his* Budget Europe *guides.*

## Fodor's Travel Guides
*The books highlight individual cities and countries. This could be of more help if you are only planning on seeing one or two cities on your trip.*

## Ford's Freighter Travel Guide

## Frommer's Guides
*An excellent choice for budget-minded travelers.*

## Gault Millau Guides
*Refreshing, critical, and honest remarks are the trademark for this series.*

### The Global Adventurer's Handbook
*John Malarkey, master adventure-traveler, gives his tips on how to plan, pay for, and enjoy your extended vacation. Contact Perpetual Press at 1-800-807-3030.*

### Going Places: The Guide to Travel Guides
*A great book that lists and describes thousands of travel guides. There are comprehensive reviews on all the popular guides as well as many that you never heard of.*

### Guide to Greater London: Hotels, Pubs, and Restaurants

### Hippocrene Books, Inc.
*They publish travel reference books, travel guides, maps, and foreign language dictionaries.*

### The Insult Dictionary: How to Give 'Em Hell in Five Different Languages
*For those times when you need to chew someone out in French, German, Italian, Spanish, and English.*

### John Muir Publications
*They publish a whole line of travel books.*

### Lonely Planet Publications
*They offer a large selection of travel books.*

### The Lover's Dictionary: How to be Amourous in Five Delectable Languages
*For those times when you need to say something romantic in French, German, Italian, Spanish, and English.*

### Moon Handbooks
*This series is for the adventurous. Public transportation is the primary mode of travel for the users of these books.*

### Passport to Discount Travel
*A great book that will help you save money.*

### Traveler's Hotline Directory
*This book lists over 12,000 toll free phone numbers for the travel industry.*

### Vagabonding USA: A Guide to Independent Travel
*One of my personal favorites. This book is a must if you are traveling around the United States.*

## TRAVEL BOOKSTORES AND MAIL ORDER COMPANIES

**Adventures Cafe**
414 K Street, Anchorage, AK 99501 ..................................... (907) 276-8282

**Basically Books**
160 Kamehameha Avenue, Hilo, HI 96720 ......................... (808) 961-0144

**Book Passage**
51 Tamal Vista Boulevard, Corte Madera, CA 94925 ........ (415) 927-0960

**California Map & Travel Center**
3312 Pico & 33rd, Santa Monica, CA 90405 ........................ (310) 829-6277

**The Complete Traveler**
3207 Filmore Street, San Francisco, CA 94123 ................... (415) 923-1511

**Complete Traveller**
199 Madison Avenue, New York, NY 10016 ....................... (212) 685-9007

**Delorme's Map Store**
2 Delorme Drive, Yarmouth, ME 04096 ............................. (207) 865-4171

**Distant Lands**
56 S Raymond Avenue, Old Pasadena, CA 91105 ............. (818) 449-3220

**Easy Going**
1385 Shattuck Avenue, Berkeley, CA 94109 ....................... (510) 843-3533
1617 Locust Street, Walnut Creek, CA 94596 .................... (510) 947-6660

**Forsyth Travel Bookstore**
226 Westchester Avenue, White Plains, NY 10604 ........... (914) 681-7235

**4 Corners Map & Travel Shop**
1887 W Market Street, Akron, OH 43313 ............................ (330) 869-6277

**Geographia Map & Travel Bookstore**
4000 Riverside Drive, Burbank, CA 91505 ......................... (818) 848-1414

**Complete Traveler**
2860 University Avenue, Madison, WI 53705 .................... (608) 233-7222

**Explore**
620 W Lincolnway, Ames, IA 50010 ................................... (515) 232-8843

**Hagstrom Map & Travel Center**
57 W 43rd Street, New York, NY 10036 ............................. (212) 398-1222

**Hannslik & Wegner International Bookstore**
20 Railroad Place, Westport, CT 06880 .............................. (203) 454-7750

**The Happy Wanderer**
320 N Highway 89A #H, Sedona, AZ 86336 ...................... (520) 282-4690

**International Travel Service**
3063 Beacon Avenue S, Seattle, WA 98144 .......................... (206) 860-5008

**Jet-Setter**
66 Laurier Street W, Montreal, PQ H2T 2N4 ..................... (514) 271-5058

**Kopi—A Traveler's Cafe**
5317 N Clark, Chicago, IL 60640 .......................................... (773) 989-5674

**Le Travel Store**
745 4th Avenue, San Diego, CA 92101 ................................ (619) 544-0005

**The Map Center**
63 Washington Street, Santa Clara, CA 95050 .................... (408) 296-6277
2440 Bancroft Way, Berkeley, CA 94704 ............................. (510) 841-6277

**Map Centre Inc.**
2611 University Avenue, San Diego, CA 92104 ................. (619) 291-3830

**The Map Man**
17 W Nicholai, Hicksville, NY 11801 ................................. (516) 931-8404

**The Map Shop**
5-B E Coffee Street, Greenville, SC 29602 .......................... (864) 271-6277

**The Map Store**
200 S 6th Street, Minneapolis, MN 55402 .......................... (612) 339-4117
5821 Karric Square Drive, Dublin, OH 43016 .................... (614) 792-6277
30 E 7th Street, Saint Paul, MN 55101 ................................ (612) 227-6277
1636 Eye Street NW, Washington, DC 20006 ..................... (202) 628-2608

**Maps Unlimited**
800 Lincoln, Denver, CO 80203 ........................................... (303) 623-4299
9955 East Hampton, Denver, CO 80231

**Metsker Maps of Bellevue**
14150 NE 20th, Bellevue, WA 98005 .................................... (425) 746-3200

**Metsker Maps of Seattle**
702 1st Avenue, Seattle, WA 98104 ..................................... (206) 623-8747

**Metsker Maps of Tacoma**
6249 Tacoma Mall Boulevard, Tacoma, WA 98409

**Pacific Travellers Supply**
12 W Anapanu Street, Santa Barbara, CA 93101 ............... (805) 963-4438

**Passenger Stop—Your Travel Store**
812 Kenilworth Drive, Towson, MD 21208 ........................ (800) 261-5888
(410) 821-5888

**Phileas Fogg's Books**
87 Stanford Shopping Center, Palo Alto, CA 94304 .......... (650) 327-1754

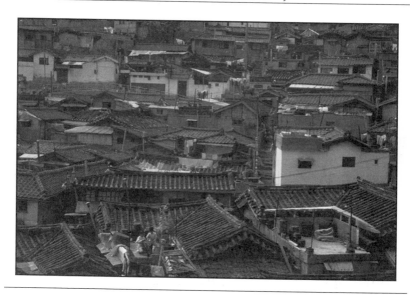

### Powell's Travel Store
701 SW Sixth Avenue, Portland, OR 97204 ........................ (503) 228-1108

### Rand McNally Map & Travel Store (www.randmcnally.com)
3333 Bristol Street, Suite 2231, Costa Mesa, CA 92626 ..... (714) 545-9907
243 Horton Plaza, San Diego, CA 92101 ............................. (619) 234-3341
595 Market Street, San Francisco, CA 94105 ...................... (415) 777-3131
3101 PGA Boulevard, Palm Beach Gardens, FL 33410 ..... (561) 775-7602
444 N Michigan Avenue, Chicago, IL 60601 ...................... (312) 321-1751
452 Oakbrook Center, Oak Brook, IL 60521 ...................... (630) 571-3006
84 State Street, Boston, MA 02109 ....................................... (617) 720-1125
7101 Democracy Boulevard, Bethesda, MD 20817 ........... (301) 365-6277
Sommerset Collection .......................................................... (248) 643-7470
   2801 W Big Beaver Road J226, Troy, MI 48084
2423 St. Louis Galleria, St. Louis, MO 63117 ...................... (314) 863-3555
150 E 52nd Street, New York, NY 10022 ............................. (212) 758-7488
1650 Market Street, Suite 100, Philadelphia, PA 19103 ..... (215) 563-1101
200 North Park Center, Dallas, TX 75225 .......................... (214) 987-9941
5015 Westheimer, Houston, TX 77056 ................................ (713) 960-9846
7988 Tysons Corner Center, McLean, VA 22102 ................ (703) 556-8688
150 S Wacker, Chicago, IL 60606 ........................................ (312) 332-2009

### The Savvy Traveler
310 South Michigan, Chicago, IL 60604 .............................. (312) 913-9800

**Thomas Brothers Maps**
521 W 6th Street, Los Angeles, CA 90017 ............................ (213) 627-4018
17731 Cowan, Irvine, CA 92714 ............................................ (714) 863-1984
550 Jackson Street, San Francisco, CA 94133 ...................... (415) 981-7520

**Travel & Nature**
59 Water Street, Exeter, NH 03833 ...................................... (603) 772-5573

**Travel Books & Language Center**
4437 Wisconsin Avenue NW, Washington, DC 20016 ...... (301) 951-8533

**The Travel Bug**
2667 W Broadway, Vancouver, BC V6K 2G2 ...................... (604) 737-1122

**The Travel Emporium**
210 Ventura Boulevard, Woodland Hills, CA 91364 ......... (818) 592-0718

**The Travel Gallery**
1007 Manhattan Avenue, Manhattan Beach, CA 90266 .... (310) 379-9199

**The Travel Store**
56 1/2 N Santa Cruz Avenue, Los Gatos, CA 95030 ......... (408) 354-9909

**Traveler's Depot**
1655 Garnet Avenue, San Diego, CA 92109 ........................ (619) 483-1421

**Traveller's Bookstore**
22 W 52nd Street, New York, NY 10020 ....................... (800) 755-TRAVEL
(212) 664-0995

**Ulysses Travel Books & Maps**
4176 Saint Denis, Montreal, PQ H2W 2M5 ........................ (514) 843-9447
4 Rana Lavasqua, Quebec City, PQ G1R 2B1 .................... (418) 529-5349
101 Yorkville Avenue, Toronto, ON M5R 1C1 ................... (416) 323-3609

**Venture Map & Globe**
2525 W Anderson, Suite 225, Austin, TX 78757 ................ (512) 452-2326

**Wanderlust**
1929 W 4th Street, Vancouver, BC V6J 1M7 ...................... (604) 739-2182

**Wide World Books & Maps**
1911 N 45th Street, Seattle, WA 98103 ............................... (206) 634-3453

**Wide World of Maps**
2626 W Indian School Road, Phoenix, AZ 85017 .............. (602) 279-2323
1334 S Country Club Drive, Mesa, AZ 85210 .................... (602) 844-1134

**Woodruff & Blum Booksellers**
Samson Mall, P.O. Box 118,
Lake Louise, Alberta, TOL 1EO ....................................... (403) 522-3842

**World Wide Books & Maps**
736 Granville Street, Vancouver, BC V6Z 1G3 .................. (604) 687-3320

# INDEX

# ORDER FORM
## (This form may be photocopied)

"Enterprising travelers should consider flying as a courier. Check out Mark I. Field's travel handbook."
*–Let's Go Travel Guides*

To order additional copies of *The Courier Air Travel Handbook*, or to check on the availability of our other travel and employment titles, fill out the form below or call:

## (800) 807-3030

(Credit card orders only)

Send check or money order with this form to:
**PERPETUAL PRESS**
P.O. Box 30413
Lansing, MI 48909-7913

____ copies of the Courier Handbook @ $9.95 each [        ]

Shipping and handling @ $3.00 each [        ]

TOTAL [        ]

## SHIPPING INFORMATION

Name: _____

Address: _____

City/State/Zip: _____

Phone: _____

Email Address: _____